AI for Business

A Practical Guide to AI-Powered Productivity

Ken Tannenbaum

2026

Finnoybu Press

AI for Business

2026 Edition

A Practical Guide to AI-Powered Productivity

Published by Finnoybu Press

For permissions and inquiries: press@finnoybu.org

First Edition: 2026

About the Author

Ken Tannenbaum is a technologist, entrepreneur, and AI governance researcher. He is the founder of Finnoybu Press and the founder/steward of the AEGIS Initiative, an open framework for AI safety and accountability. Learn more at aegis-initiative.com.

When he's not building governance standards for artificial intelligence, he's helping everyday people understand and use it.

Dedication

To every professional who has ever stared at a blank screen, an overflowing inbox, or a spreadsheet full of numbers that refuse to tell a story — help has arrived.

And to the IT departments everywhere who are about to get a lot more questions.

The AI for Everyone Series

This book is part of the **AI for Everyone** series by Finnoybu Press, designed to help real people use AI tools effectively. Visit **press.finnoybu.org** for the latest titles and updates.

Collection One: Product Deep Dives

- *ChatGPT: The Definitive Guide (2026 Edition)*
- *ChatGPT: The Power User Guide (2026 Edition)*
- *Claude: The Definitive Guide (2026 Edition)*
- *Claude Code: The Power User Guide (2026 Edition)*
- *Gemini: The Complete Guide (2026 Edition)*
- *Gemini: The Advanced Guide (2026 Edition)*
- *Copilot: The Workplace AI Guide (2026 Edition)*
- *Copilot: The Advanced Workplace Guide (2026 Edition)*
- *Perplexity: The Research Playbook (2026 Edition)*
- *Perplexity: The Advanced Research Playbook (2026 Edition)*

Collection Two: Product Guides

- *NotebookLM: From Sources to Audio Overviews (2026 Edition)*
- *DeepSeek: Code, Math, and Reasoning (2026 Edition)*
- *Cursor: The AI Code Editor (2026 Edition)*
- *OpenClaw: Agentic AI for Everyday Work (2026 Edition)*

Collection Three: Cross-Platform Skills

- *AI Systems Playbook (2026 Edition)*
- *AI Prompt Engineering (2026 Edition)*
- *AI for Developers (2026 Edition)*
- *AI for Business (2026 Edition)*
- *AI for Students (2026 Edition)*
- *AI Governance for Practitioners (2026 Edition)*
- *Securing Agentic AI (2026 Edition)*

Table of Contents

Introduction: Why This Book Exists

You are busy. Your inbox has 47 unread messages. You have a quarterly report due Friday, a presentation to the board next Tuesday, and somewhere in the chaos of your calendar, you are supposed to be "thinking strategically about the future of the business."

Meanwhile, everyone is talking about AI. Your CEO mentioned it at the last all-hands. Your competitors are slapping "AI-powered" on everything. LinkedIn is full of people claiming they 10x'd their productivity with a single prompt. Your twenty-something colleague mentions, casually, that they "had Claude write the first draft" of a market analysis, and you are not entirely sure whether to be impressed or concerned.

Here is what I know about you: you do not need another breathless article about how AI will change everything. You need to know what it can do for you, specifically, starting this week.

That is what this book is for.

Who This Book Is For

This book is written for people who work in business — broadly defined. That includes:

- **Managers and team leads** who need to produce more with the same resources and are wondering whether AI can help or whether it is just another tool that creates more work than it saves
- **Individual contributors** — analysts, marketers, project managers, HR professionals, salespeople — who want to work faster and produce higher-quality output
- **Entrepreneurs and small business owners** who are effectively a one-person marketing department, sales team, HR department, and strategic planning committee, and who could use a capable assistant that works at 3 AM without complaining
- **Executives** who need to understand what AI can realistically deliver so they can make informed decisions about adoption, investment, and policy

- **Teams** trying to incorporate AI into existing workflows without creating chaos

If you use a computer for work and you produce some combination of emails, documents, spreadsheets, presentations, and decisions, this book has something for you.

What This Book Is Not

Let me be direct about what you will not find here.

This is not a technical book. You do not need to understand neural networks, transformer architectures, or the technical difference between GPT-5.5 and Claude Sonnet. When technical details matter for a business decision, I will explain them plainly. Otherwise, I will skip them.

This is not a hype piece. I am not going to tell you that AI will solve all your problems, replace half your workforce, or transform your business overnight. Some AI evangelists have done real damage by overpromising. I would rather give you an honest, practical perspective that helps you make good decisions.

This is not a book about a single AI product. If you want a deep dive into ChatGPT, Claude, Gemini, or Copilot, I have written dedicated guides for each (see the series listing). This book is about using AI strategically across your business, regardless of which tools you choose.

This is not a book about building AI products. If you are an engineer looking to integrate AI into your company's software, you need a different book. This one is about using AI as a business professional to do your existing job better.

What This Book Is

This book is a practical, department-by-department, task-by-task guide to using AI effectively in a business context. Here is what you will walk away with:

A realistic understanding of what AI can and cannot do in 2026. The capabilities are impressive, but they have real limitations. Knowing both sides is what separates effective AI users from people who waste time or, worse, create problems.

Specific techniques for your actual work. Not abstract concepts — concrete approaches for writing emails, analyzing data, preparing for meetings, building presentations, conducting research, and dozens of other tasks you do every week.

Prompt templates you can use immediately. Throughout the book and in the appendices, you will find ready-to-use prompts for common business tasks. Copy them, modify them, and make them your own.

A framework for choosing the right tools. There are now several excellent AI platforms, each with different strengths. I will help you figure out which ones are worth your time and money based on what you need to accomplish.

A strategy for AI adoption. Whether you are rolling out AI to a team of five or an organization of five thousand, you need a thoughtful approach. I will give you one that works.

Honest guidance on privacy, security, and ethics. These are not afterthoughts — they are central to using AI responsibly in a business context. Your legal team will thank you for reading those chapters.

How to Read This Book

You have two options, and both are valid.

Option 1: Read it straight through. The book is structured to build on itself. Early chapters establish foundations, middle chapters cover specific business functions, and later chapters address organizational and strategic concerns. If you are new to AI in business, this is the way to go.

Option 2: Jump to what you need. Each chapter is designed to stand on its own. If you are a marketer who needs help with content strategy right now, skip to Chapter 10. If your boss just asked you to evaluate AI tools for the team, go to Chapter 2. The table of contents is organized by business function for this reason.

Either way, I recommend at least skimming Chapters 1 through 3 first. They provide context that will make everything else more useful.

A Note About Accuracy

The AI landscape changes constantly. New models launch monthly, features get added, prices shift, and best practices evolve. This book is accurate as of May

2026, but specific details — vendor pricing, feature availability, exact tool capabilities — may have shifted by the time you read this.

The principles, techniques, and strategies in this book have a much longer shelf life than the tool details. How to communicate effectively with AI, evaluate output critically, and integrate AI into business workflows responsibly — those skills transfer across versions and across tools.

When something seems different from what's described here, check the vendor's documentation for the latest information.

Let's Get Started

You picked up this book because you want to work smarter, not because you want to become an AI expert. Good. That is exactly the right motivation.

By the time you finish — or, more realistically, by the time you finish the first few chapters relevant to your role — you should be saving real time on real work. Not theoretical time. Not "if everything goes perfectly" time. Actual, measurable time you can spend on the work that requires your uniquely human judgment, creativity, and expertise.

That is the promise of AI in business done right. Not replacing you. Amplifying you.

Let's get to it.

Part I: The Business Case for AI

"The greatest danger in times of turbulence is not the turbulence; it is to act with yesterday's logic."

— Peter Drucker

Chapter 1: AI at Work in 2026

If you had told a business professional in 2022 that within four years they would be routinely asking an AI to draft their emails, analyze their spreadsheets, summarize their meetings, and help them think through strategic decisions, most would have called you optimistic. Yet here we are.

The AI landscape in 2026 looks nothing like the one that existed when ChatGPT appeared in late 2022 and briefly became the fastest-growing consumer application in history. What started as a novelty — a chatbot that could write passable poetry and questionable code — has matured into a real business tool. Several of them.

But maturity has not brought clarity. If anything, the proliferation of AI tools, the constant drumbeat of product announcements, and the wildly divergent claims about AI's potential have made it harder for business professionals to separate signal from noise.

Let us start there.

What AI Can Actually Do in 2026

Here is a grounded assessment of where AI capabilities stand as of early 2026, specifically for business applications.

Language tasks are excellent. The current generation of large language models — GPT-5.5 and its predecessors from OpenAI, Claude from Anthropic, Gemini from Google — are remarkably good at understanding and generating business language. They draft emails that sound natural, summarize 30-page reports into crisp executive briefs, rewrite content for different audiences, and produce first drafts of everything from job descriptions to marketing copy. This is not a future promise. It works now, and it works well.

Analysis has become practical. AI can now meaningfully engage with business data. Upload a spreadsheet, and the leading tools will identify trends, create visualizations, flag anomalies, and answer questions about the data in plain English. The analysis is not always perfect — you still need to verify conclusions — but it is fast, and often insightful. For the business professional who is not a data scientist but needs to make sense of numbers, this is transformative.

Multimodal capabilities are real. Modern AI does not just work with text. You can upload images, charts, PDFs, and photographs, and the AI will understand and reason about them. Need to extract data from a photographed whiteboard? Compare two versions of a design mockup? Pull numbers from a scanned invoice? Routine tasks now.

Integration with existing tools is happening. Microsoft Copilot is embedded in Microsoft 365. Google's Gemini lives inside Workspace. These are not bolt-on accessories — they are woven into the tools you already use, which dramatically lowers the friction of adoption.

Reasoning capabilities have improved significantly. The latest models work through multi-step problems, consider tradeoffs, evaluate options against criteria you specify, and engage in something that resembles strategic thinking. They are not infallible, but they are useful thinking partners.

What AI Still Cannot Do

Here is where honesty matters more than enthusiasm.

AI does not know your business. It can analyze the data you give it and apply general business knowledge, but it does not know your company's culture, history, internal politics, customer relationships, or the dozen contextual factors that inform every important decision. You bring that context. AI helps you process it.

AI makes things up. The technical term is "hallucination," and it has not been fully solved in 2026. AI will occasionally present fabricated information with complete confidence — citing studies that do not exist, inventing statistics, or confusing details between similar topics. This happens less than it did in 2023, but it still happens. Every factual claim in AI-generated content needs verification, especially in high-stakes contexts like legal, financial, or medical domains.

AI cannot replace judgment. It can help you think through a decision by presenting options, identifying risks, and even playing devil's advocate. But the actual decision — the one that accounts for ethics, relationships, timing, organizational politics, and your own values — is still yours to make. And it should be.

AI is not creative the way humans are. It can generate novel combinations of existing ideas, and sometimes those combinations are useful. But breakthrough creativity — the kind that comes from lived experience, emotional insight, and the willingness to be wrong in interesting ways — remains human territory.

AI cannot reliably handle complex, multi-step processes without oversight. Despite progress in "agentic" AI — systems that take a series of actions independently — the technology is not reliable enough for high-stakes, fully autonomous workflows. Think of AI as a capable assistant that still needs supervision, not an employee you can set loose.

The Business AI Landscape

Let me give you a quick orientation to the major players, which we will explore in much more detail in Chapter 2.

OpenAI (ChatGPT, GPT-5.5, GPT-5.5 Thinking) remains the most widely recognized name in AI. The product line has expanded significantly, with different models optimized for different tasks — some for speed and cost, others for deep reasoning. ChatGPT is available as a free tier, a Plus subscription, and a Team/Enterprise tier with business-specific features.

Anthropic (Claude) has positioned itself as the thinking person's AI. Claude's strengths are nuanced writing, careful analysis, and handling long documents — it works with up to a million tokens of context in a single conversation. Anthropic's focus on AI safety produces a model less likely to generate problematic content, which matters in professional settings.

Google (Gemini) has the deepest integration with the tools many businesses already use. If your organization runs on Google Workspace, Gemini's native integration with Gmail, Docs, Sheets, and the rest of the suite makes it a natural choice. Gemini also has strong multimodal capabilities and benefits from Google's data infrastructure.

Microsoft (Copilot) follows the same logic for Microsoft shops. If your business lives in Microsoft 365 — Word, Excel, PowerPoint, Outlook, Teams —

Copilot brings AI directly into those workflows. The integration is its primary selling point.

Perplexity has carved out a niche as an AI-powered research tool. It combines AI reasoning with real-time web search and returns sourced answers, making it useful for market research, competitive analysis, and fact-checking.

These are not the only AI tools available, but they are the ones that matter most for general business productivity in 2026. Specialized tools exist for specific functions — AI-powered CRMs, design tools, coding assistants — and we will touch on those in the relevant chapters.

How Businesses Are Actually Using AI

Here is what I am seeing in practice, based on real-world adoption patterns rather than vendor marketing.

The Quick Wins

Most businesses start with the obvious stuff — tasks where AI delivers clear, immediate value with minimal risk:

- **Email drafting and response.** This is often the gateway. Someone uses ChatGPT or Claude to draft a difficult email and realizes it took two minutes instead of twenty. Then they use it for the next email, and the next, and suddenly it is part of their workflow.
- **Meeting summaries.** AI tools that join meetings and produce summaries with action items have seen massive adoption. The time savings are obvious and the risk is low.
- **Document summarization.** Drop a 50-page RFP into Claude and ask for a summary of key requirements. What used to take an hour takes five minutes.
- **First drafts.** Reports, proposals, job descriptions, social media posts, internal communications — anything where the blank page is the hardest part.

The Intermediate Applications

As comfort grows, businesses move into more substantive applications:

- **Data analysis.** Uploading spreadsheets and asking AI to identify patterns, create charts, and flag outliers.
- **Competitive research.** Using Perplexity or ChatGPT to quickly synthesize information about competitors, market trends, and industry developments.
- **Content strategy.** Not just writing individual pieces, but using AI to plan editorial calendars, analyze content performance, and identify gaps.
- **Customer communication templates.** Developing AI-assisted response templates for common customer scenarios.

The Advanced Use Cases

A smaller but growing number of businesses use AI for strategic work:

- **Scenario planning.** Using AI to model different strategic options and stress-test assumptions.
- **Process design.** Building AI-powered workflows that automate multi-step business processes.
- **Knowledge management.** Creating AI-accessible repositories of institutional knowledge that make it easier for anyone in the organization to find and apply what the company collectively knows.

The Productivity Reality Check

Here is the question everyone wants answered: how much time does AI actually save?

The honest answer is that it depends on what you do, how you adopt it, and whether you are measuring the right things. But here are some real numbers from studies and surveys conducted in 2025:

- **Writing tasks** see the most consistent improvement. Most professionals report saving 30 to 50 percent of the time they would normally spend on writing-heavy tasks. For some tasks — like drafting routine correspondence — the savings can approach 70 to 80 percent.
- **Research tasks** typically see 40 to 60 percent time savings, with the caveat that you need to verify AI-gathered information, which eats into some of those gains.

- **Data analysis** is harder to quantify because AI often enables analysis that would not have happened at all. A marketing manager who would never have built a cohort analysis in Excel might now do it routinely with AI assistance.
- **Meeting-related tasks** — prep, notes, follow-ups — see roughly 25 to 40 percent time savings.

These are averages. Your mileage will vary based on your work, your prompt skills, and which tools you use. Chapter 3 will help you measure your own ROI.

The Job Question

I know it is on your mind, so let me address it directly: is AI going to take your job?

For the overwhelming majority of business professionals reading this book, the answer is no — but AI will change your job. The nature of your work will shift. Tasks that used to consume hours will take minutes. Skills that used to be differentiators — like the ability to write a clean first draft quickly — will become table stakes. New skills — directing AI effectively, critically evaluating its output, integrating it into workflows — will become the new differentiators.

The professionals who thrive will be the ones who learn to work with AI effectively, not the ones who try to compete with it on tasks it does well, and not the ones who ignore it out of discomfort or principle.

AI is not replacing managers, analysts, marketers, or salespeople. It is replacing the tedious parts of those jobs and raising the bar for the strategic, creative, and relational parts.

That is not a threat. That is an upgrade.

What You Need to Get Started

The barrier to entry is remarkably low. Here is what you need:

1. **An account on at least one major AI platform.** ChatGPT, Claude, and Gemini all offer free tiers sufficient to start. Paid tiers (typically $20 per month) unlock significantly more capability.

2. **A willingness to experiment.** AI is a tool you learn by using. No amount of reading about it substitutes for sitting down and trying it with your real work.
3. **A healthy dose of skepticism.** Trust but verify. AI is useful precisely because it is fast, but speed without accuracy is worse than useless.
4. **This book.** I will walk you through specific, practical applications for your work. By the time you finish the chapters relevant to your role, you will have a clear picture of where AI fits into your workflow and how to get the most out of it.

Let's start with the most important practical decision: which AI tools are right for your business.

Chapter 2: Choosing the Right AI for Your Business

You do not need every AI tool on the market. You probably do not need most of them. But you do need to understand what is available so you can make an informed decision about where to invest your time and your company's money.

This chapter is not an exhaustive product review — it is a buyer's guide. I will tell you what each major platform is good at, where it falls short, what it costs, and who should be using it. By the end, you should have a clear idea of which one or two tools deserve your attention.

The Big Five for Business

As of early 2026, five AI platforms matter for general business productivity. There are dozens of specialized tools for specific functions — I will mention some in the relevant chapters — but these five cover the broadest range of business use cases.

ChatGPT (OpenAI)

What it is: The most widely used AI assistant in the world, available via web, desktop, and mobile apps.

What it is good at: - General-purpose business writing across every format you can think of - Code generation and technical problem-solving (relevant if you work with data, spreadsheets, or light automation) - Image generation via DALL-E (useful for marketing and presentations) - Voice conversations (the mobile app lets you talk to ChatGPT naturally, which is surprisingly useful for brainstorming) - Plugin and GPT ecosystem (custom AI assistants built for specific tasks) - Broad general knowledge and strong reasoning, especially with the GPT-5.5 Thinking model

Where it falls short: - Can be verbose — it tends to over-explain and pad responses unless you ask it not to - The free tier is increasingly limited; the real value is in the paid plans - Enterprise data privacy requires the Team or

Enterprise tier — the free and Plus tiers may use your data for training - Occasional confidence in wrong answers, particularly for niche or technical topics

What it costs: - Free tier: Limited GPT-5.5 access, limited messages per day - Plus ($20/month): Full GPT-5.5 access, reasoning models, image generation, file uploads - Team ($25/user/month): Plus features with workspace management and better data privacy - Enterprise (custom pricing): Full data privacy, admin controls, SSO, higher limits

Best for: Generalists who need a versatile tool for a wide range of tasks. The default choice if you are only going to use one AI platform.

Claude (Anthropic)

What it is: An AI assistant known for nuanced thinking, careful writing, and the ability to work with extremely long documents.

What it is good at: - Long-form writing that sounds natural and thoughtful rather than robotic - Analyzing lengthy documents — contracts, reports, research papers — Claude handles up to a million tokens of context, roughly 750,000 words - Careful, nuanced reasoning that considers multiple perspectives - Following complex instructions precisely - Being appropriately cautious — it will tell you when it is uncertain rather than making something up - Coding and technical analysis

Where it falls short: - No native image generation (it can analyze images but not create them) - Smaller plugin/integration ecosystem compared to ChatGPT - Can sometimes be overly cautious or hedge more than necessary - Less name recognition, which means fewer community resources and tutorials

What it costs: - Free tier: Limited Claude Sonnet access - Pro ($20/month): Extended Claude Sonnet and Opus access, file uploads, longer conversations - Team ($25/user/month): Pro features with team management - Enterprise (custom pricing): SSO, enhanced security, higher usage limits

Best for: Professionals who work primarily with text — writers, analysts, strategists, lawyers, consultants. If your work involves thinking carefully and producing polished written output, Claude is hard to beat.

Gemini (Google)

What it is: Google's AI assistant, available standalone and deeply integrated into Google Workspace.

What it is good at: - Native Google Workspace integration — it works directly inside Gmail, Docs, Sheets, Slides, and Meet - Real-time information access via Google Search integration - Multimodal capabilities — particularly strong with image understanding and video - Processing and summarizing content across your Google Drive - Strong analytical capabilities, especially when working with data in Google Sheets

Where it falls short: - Writing quality can feel more mechanical than Claude or ChatGPT - The Workspace integration, while useful, can feel limited in what it actually automates - Gemini's standalone experience is less polished than ChatGPT's - Pricing is bundled with Workspace in ways that can be confusing

What it costs: - Free tier: Basic Gemini access via gemini.google.com - Google AI Plus ($7.99/month) and Pro ($19.99/month): Advanced Gemini access with storage and Workspace integration - Google AI Ultra ($249.99/month): Top-tier access with the largest usage limits - Workspace add-on (varies): Gemini for Workspace pricing depends on your existing plan

Best for: Teams already on Google Workspace. The integration advantage is real — if your company runs on Gmail, Google Docs, and Google Sheets, Gemini's native presence in those tools reduces friction significantly.

Microsoft Copilot

What it is: AI deeply embedded in Microsoft 365 — Word, Excel, PowerPoint, Outlook, and Teams.

What it is good at: - Working directly within Microsoft Office applications you already use every day - Excel analysis and formula generation — genuinely useful for spreadsheet-heavy roles - PowerPoint creation from prompts or documents - Email drafting and summarization in Outlook - Meeting summaries and action items in Teams - Enterprise-grade security and compliance (inherits your Microsoft 365 security posture)

Where it falls short: - Requires a Microsoft 365 subscription as a prerequisite — you cannot use Copilot without it - The per-user cost is high, especially for smaller teams - Quality of output can be inconsistent — some tasks work beautifully, others feel half-baked - The AI sometimes struggles with complex or nuanced requests compared to standalone tools

What it costs: - Copilot (free): Basic AI assistant in Bing and Windows, limited capabilities - Copilot Pro ($20/month): Enhanced AI in Microsoft 365 apps for individuals - Microsoft 365 Copilot Business ($18–21/user/month) and Enterprise ($30/user/month): Full business integration, requires a Microsoft 365 business plan - E7 Frontier Suite ($99/user/month): Top-tier capabilities including Agent 365 ($15/mo standalone)

Best for: Microsoft-centric organizations, especially those with existing Microsoft 365 E3 or E5 plans. The integration with Excel, PowerPoint, and Teams is the main draw. If your team already pays for Microsoft 365, adding Copilot is a natural extension.

Perplexity

What it is: An AI-powered research and answer engine that combines AI reasoning with real-time web search.

What it is good at: - Research that requires current, sourced information — every answer includes citations - Market research and competitive analysis - Fact-checking and verification - Quick answers to specific business questions with links to sources - Staying current — it searches the web in real time, so answers reflect the latest information

Where it falls short: - Not designed for content generation — it is a research tool, not a writing tool - Limited document handling compared to ChatGPT or Claude - No integration with business productivity suites - The free tier is useful but caps Pro searches per day

What it costs: - Free tier: Basic searches with standard AI - Pro ($20/month): More searches, advanced AI models, file uploads - Enterprise ($40/user/month): Team features, API access, enhanced privacy

Best for: Anyone who does regular research — analysts, strategists, marketers, consultants. Not a replacement for ChatGPT or Claude, but an excellent complement.

How to Choose: A Decision Framework

Here is my practical advice for choosing the right AI tools for your business.

If you are an individual professional picking one tool:

Start with **ChatGPT Plus** or **Claude Pro**. Both cost $20 per month, both are excellent for general business tasks, and both will serve you well for most use cases in this book.

Choose ChatGPT if you want the broadest range of capabilities (writing, images, voice, plugins) and the largest ecosystem of tutorials and community resources.

Choose Claude if you work primarily with text — if your job involves a lot of writing, reading, analysis, and thinking. Claude tends to produce more natural writing and handle nuance better.

If you are choosing for a team:

Start with what you already pay for. If your organization runs Microsoft 365, evaluate Copilot. If you run Google Workspace, evaluate Gemini. The integration advantage is meaningful — people are more likely to use AI when it appears in the tools they already have open.

Add a standalone tool for power users. Even if you adopt Copilot or Gemini organization-wide, your most AI-forward team members will benefit from a standalone tool like ChatGPT or Claude for tasks requiring more sophisticated interaction.

Consider Perplexity for research-heavy roles. If your analysts, strategists, or marketers spend significant time on research, Perplexity's sourced-answer approach is worth the investment.

If budget is a constraint:

The free tiers are more capable than you might expect. A small business or startup can accomplish a lot with free ChatGPT, free Claude, and free Perplexity. You will hit usage limits and miss some advanced features, but you can still save meaningful time.

When you are ready to upgrade, start with one paid subscription ($20/month) and expand based on demonstrated value. Chapter 3 will help you measure it.

The Multi-Tool Approach

Vendor marketing will never tell you this: most power users do not rely on a single AI tool. They use different tools for different tasks based on each tool's strengths.

A common setup for a well-equipped business professional in 2026:

- **Claude** for writing, analysis, and deep thinking tasks
- **ChatGPT** for quick tasks, image generation, and voice brainstorming
- **Perplexity** for research and fact-finding
- **Copilot or Gemini** for tasks within their respective office suites

This approach costs roughly $60 to $80 per month across subscriptions, which sounds like a lot until you calculate the hours saved. If these tools save you even five hours per month — and they will almost certainly save more — the effective hourly cost makes this an easy decision.

What About Specialized AI Tools?

Beyond the Big Five, there are hundreds of AI tools designed for specific business functions:

- **Jasper** and **Copy.ai** for marketing content
- **Otter.ai** and **Fireflies** for meeting transcription and notes
- **Beautiful.ai** and **Gamma** for AI-powered presentations
- **Notion AI** for workspace and project management
- **HubSpot AI** and **Salesforce Einstein** for CRM and sales
- **Grammarly** for writing polish and tone adjustment

My advice: start with the general-purpose platforms. They handle 80 percent of use cases well. Adopt specialized tools only when you have identified a specific gap the general-purpose tools cannot fill, and when the specialized tool delivers enough additional value to justify the cost and complexity of another tool in your stack.

Data Privacy: The Question You Must Ask

Before committing to any AI platform for business use, you need to understand one thing: what happens to the data you share with it?

This is not a theoretical concern. When you paste a confidential financial report into an AI chat, upload a customer list, or discuss an unreleased product strategy — where does that information go? Can it be used to train the AI model? Could it surface in someone else's conversation?

Here are the key distinctions:

Free tiers of most AI platforms may use your interactions to train future models. Information you share could, in theory, influence the model's future responses. For casual personal use, this is fine. For confidential business data, it is a problem.

Paid individual tiers vary by provider. Most paid plans offer the option to opt out of training data use, though some — notably Anthropic's consumer plans as of August 2025 — opt you in by default. Verify current terms, as policies evolve.

Business and Enterprise tiers universally promise that your data will not be used for model training. If you handle sensitive business information — and you almost certainly do — this is the tier you need.

Microsoft Copilot and Google Gemini for Workspace inherit your existing Microsoft or Google security infrastructure, a significant advantage for organizations that already have enterprise agreements with these vendors.

We will go deeper on privacy and security in Chapter 21, but here is the bottom line: do not put confidential business data into the free tier of any AI tool. Period.

My Recommendation

If I had to give you a single sentence of advice, it would be this: start with one paid subscription to either ChatGPT or Claude, use it consistently for two weeks, measure the time you save, and let the results guide your next move.

The worst decision is no decision. Every week you spend deliberating about which AI tool to try is a week you could have been saving time with any of them.

Pick one. Start using it. The next chapter will help you figure out whether it is paying off.

Chapter 3: The ROI of AI

When your CEO asks "what is the return on our AI investment?" — and they will — you need a better answer than "it feels like it saves time." This chapter gives you the framework to measure AI's impact on your business, justify the investment, and identify where to double down.

Why Measuring AI ROI Is Harder Than It Looks

AI productivity gains are real, but slippery. Unlike traditional software that automates a discrete task — "we replaced manual invoicing with automated invoicing and saved 12 hours per week" — AI's benefits are distributed across dozens of small tasks throughout the day. You draft an email in two minutes instead of ten. You summarize a report in thirty seconds instead of fifteen minutes. You prepare for a meeting in five minutes instead of thirty.

Each saving feels modest. But they compound. A professional who saves fifteen minutes per hour on AI-assisted tasks across a full workday is recovering two hours of productive time. Over a month, that is roughly forty hours — an entire work week.

The challenge is capturing those savings systematically rather than relying on gut feeling.

The Three Dimensions of AI ROI

Business value from AI comes in three forms, and most organizations only measure the first one.

Dimension 1: Time Savings

The most obvious and easiest to measure. AI helps you do existing tasks faster. Here is how to quantify it.

The Time Diary Method

For one week, track your AI-assisted tasks using a simple log:

Task	Without AI	With AI	Saved	Notes
Draft Q1 summary email	25 min	8 min	17 min	Minor edits needed
Summarize vendor proposal	45 min	5 min	40 min	Uploaded 30-page PDF
Create meeting agenda	15 min	3 min	12 min	Used past agendas as input
Analyze sales data	60 min	15 min	45 min	AI caught a trend I missed

You do not need perfect measurements. Reasonable estimates are fine. The goal is order of magnitude, not minute-precision.

After a week of tracking, multiply your daily average time savings by twenty (working days per month) to get a monthly figure. Then multiply that by your effective hourly cost to the business — not just your salary, but loaded cost including benefits, overhead, and the value of your output.

Here is a concrete example:

- Average daily time savings: 45 minutes
- Monthly savings: 45 x 20 = 900 minutes = 15 hours
- Fully loaded hourly cost: $75 (this is typical for a mid-level professional when you include benefits and overhead)
- Monthly value of time saved: $1,125
- Monthly cost of AI tools: $60 (Claude Pro + Perplexity Pro)
- **Monthly net ROI: $1,065**
- **Annual net ROI: $12,780**

For a team of ten, that is $127,800 per year in recovered productivity against roughly $7,200 in tool costs. That is a return ratio that most CFOs will approve without hesitation.

Dimension 2: Quality Improvement

Time savings are only part of the story. AI also improves the quality of your output, and this is where the harder-to-measure but often more valuable benefits live.

Fewer errors. AI catches mistakes you miss when you are rushing. A financial report reviewed by AI before submission is less likely to contain calculation errors, inconsistencies, or unclear language.

Better first impressions. A proposal drafted with AI assistance tends to be better organized, more persuasive, and more polished than a rushed first draft knocked out at 4:45 PM on a Friday. The proposal that wins the contract does not show up as "time saved" — it shows up as revenue.

More thorough analysis. Without AI, you might glance at top-line numbers in a spreadsheet. With AI, you can explore the data, identify segments, spot anomalies, and arrive at insights you would not have found otherwise. Better decisions follow from better analysis.

Consistency. AI helps maintain consistent voice, formatting, and quality across multiple documents and team members. This is particularly valuable for customer-facing communications.

Measuring quality improvement is more subjective than measuring time savings, but here are some proxies you can track:

- Revision cycles: are documents requiring fewer rounds of editing before approval?
- Error rates: are you catching fewer mistakes in final deliverables?
- Win rates: are proposals or pitches performing better?
- Customer satisfaction: are communication quality scores improving?
- Stakeholder feedback: are executives commenting on improved report quality?

Dimension 3: Capability Expansion

The most underappreciated form of AI ROI. AI does not just help you do existing tasks faster and better — it enables work you would not have done at all.

Consider these scenarios:

The marketing manager who never did competitive analysis because it took too long. With AI, she now runs a competitive scan every quarter, and her marketing strategy is noticeably sharper.

The sales rep who never personalized proposals because he was managing too many accounts. With AI drafting customized proposal sections, he now sends personalized proposals to every prospect, and his close rate has improved by 15 percent.

The HR director who wanted to update the employee handbook but it had sat on her to-do list for two years. With AI, she produced a comprehensive update in a week.

The small business owner who could not afford market research. She now uses AI and Perplexity to produce analyses that would have cost $10,000 from a consulting firm.

These are not time savings — they are new capabilities. And they often deliver the highest business value of the three dimensions. How do you measure them? You cannot calculate the time saved on something you were not doing before. Instead, measure the business outcome:

- New revenue generated from better proposals
- Risk avoided by updating compliance documents
- Strategic advantage from regular competitive analysis
- Employee satisfaction from improved onboarding materials

Building Your AI ROI Dashboard

Here is a practical framework for tracking AI value across your team or organization.

For Individual Contributors

Track weekly: - Hours saved on AI-assisted tasks - Number of tasks completed with AI assistance - One "quality win" — a specific instance where AI improved your output

Monthly, calculate: - Total hours saved - Dollar value of time saved (hours x your loaded hourly rate) - Cost of AI tools - Net ROI

For Team Managers

Track monthly: - Aggregate hours saved across the team - Number of team members actively using AI - Top use cases by frequency and impact - Quality metrics relevant to your function (error rates, revision cycles, etc.)

Quarterly, assess: - Total dollar value of productivity gains - New capabilities enabled by AI - Tool costs and per-employee spend - Areas where AI adoption is lagging and why

For Executives

Track quarterly: - Organization-wide time savings (aggregated from team reports) - Revenue impact (improved win rates, faster time to market, new capabilities) - Risk reduction (compliance, errors, consistency) - Employee satisfaction with AI tools - Total AI tool spend vs. total measured benefit

Common ROI Pitfalls

The mistakes I see organizations make repeatedly.

Pitfall 1: Counting Only Direct Time Savings

If you only measure "I did this task in 5 minutes instead of 20," you will undercount AI's value by 50 to 70 percent. Quality improvements and capability expansions are often worth more than the time savings alone.

Pitfall 2: Measuring Tool Usage Instead of Impact

"Our team sent 500 prompts last month" tells you nothing about value. What matters is whether those prompts saved time, improved quality, or enabled new work. Some of the highest-ROI AI use cases involve a single long conversation that saves hours of work. Raw usage metrics mislead.

Pitfall 3: Ignoring the Learning Curve

AI ROI is not instant. Most professionals need two to four weeks of regular use before they develop the prompting skills and workflow habits that deliver consistent value. Measure ROI in the first week and you will underestimate the long-term benefit. Give people time to learn.

Pitfall 4: Forgetting to Count the Cost of Not Adopting

In a competitive market, the relevant comparison is not "AI vs. no AI" — it is "us with AI vs. our competitors with AI." If your competitors use AI to produce better proposals, faster analysis, and more personalized customer communications, the cost of inaction grows every month.

Pitfall 5: Overcomplicating the Measurement

You do not need a six-month study with control groups and statistical significance. A simple time diary, a weekly estimate of hours saved, and a monthly check on quality metrics will tell you what you need to know. Perfect measurement is the enemy of practical insight.

Making the Business Case

If you need to justify AI investment to leadership, here is a template that works.

The one-page AI business case:

1. **Current state:** "Our team of [X] people spends approximately [Y] hours per week on tasks that AI can meaningfully accelerate, including [list 3–5 specific tasks]."

2. **Proposed investment:** "[Tool name] at $[Z]peruserpermonthfor[N]users =$ [total] per month."

3. **Expected benefit:** "Based on a [2-week/1-month] pilot, each team member saved an average of [X] hours per week, valued at $[Y]inrecoveredproductivity. Atscale, weexpectannualsavingsof$[Z]."

4. **Return ratio:** "For every $1 invested in AI tools, we expect $[X] in recovered productivity, with additional unmeasured benefits in quality improvement and capability expansion."

5. **Risk mitigation:** "We will use the [business/enterprise] tier to ensure data privacy and compliance. See Chapter 21 for our recommended AI usage policy."

6. **Recommendation:** "Approve a [3-month] pilot for [team/department] with a full ROI review at the end of the pilot period."

This is not complicated, and it does not need to be. The economics of AI tools are overwhelmingly favorable — a $20 to $30 per month tool that saves even two hours per month pays for itself several times over. The business case practically writes itself.

A Word on Intangible Benefits

Some of AI's most important business benefits resist quantification. Employee satisfaction rises when tedious tasks get automated. Decision quality improves when people have time to think instead of just react. Innovation increases when professionals have the cognitive bandwidth to consider new approaches.

These benefits are real even if you cannot put a dollar figure on them. Do not dismiss them because they do not fit on a spreadsheet.

What "Productivity" Actually Means

Something that often gets lost in ROI conversations: saving time only creates value if the saved time is used well.

If AI saves you two hours a day but you spend those two hours on social media, the ROI is zero. The real productivity gain comes when saved time is redirected to higher-value work — strategic thinking, relationship building, creative problem-solving, and the kind of deep work that moves the business forward.

When you roll out AI to your team, be intentional about what you want people to do with the time they save. The answer should not be "more of the same work, faster." It should be "better work, period."

The Bottom Line

AI tools in 2026 are cheap and effective. A $20/month subscription that saves a professional five hours per month delivers a return that is essentially impossible to beat in any other category of business software.

But measuring and communicating that return is essential — both for justifying continued investment and for identifying where AI delivers the most value so you can focus your adoption efforts.

Start tracking this week. You will be surprised by the numbers.

Part II: Communication and Documents

"The most valuable of all talents is that of never using two words when one will do."

— Thomas Jefferson

Chapter 4: Email and Communication

Email is where most professionals first discover the power of AI — and for good reason. The average business professional spends 28 percent of their workday on email. That is more than eleven hours per week reading, writing, and managing messages. If AI can make even a modest dent in that number, the impact is significant.

This chapter is not just about email. It covers the full spectrum of business communication: emails, Slack messages, internal memos, announcements, and the daily written interactions that consume so much of your professional life. AI can help with all of it, and the techniques are largely the same.

Why AI Excels at Business Email

Business email follows patterns. The angry customer response. The project status update. The polite decline. The meeting follow-up. The introduction. The request for information. The apology for the delay.

You have written thousands of these emails, and each follows a loose template you carry in your head. AI has absorbed millions of such templates from its training data. This makes it extraordinarily good at producing first drafts that are structurally sound, appropriately toned, and ready for your personal touch.

The key insight: AI does not write your emails for you. It eliminates the blank-page problem and produces a draft that is 70 to 90 percent ready. Your job shifts from writing to editing — faster, less mentally taxing, and often a better result because you are refining something rather than creating from nothing.

Drafting Emails from Scratch

Start with the most common use case: you need to write an email and you want AI to produce a first draft.

The Basic Approach

A simple prompt works for simple emails:

> Write a professional email to our vendor, Apex Supply Co., letting them know that we need to push our Q2 order back by three weeks due to a warehouse renovation. Keep the tone friendly but clear, and ask them to confirm the revised timeline.

Any major AI tool will produce a solid draft from this prompt. You can get dramatically better results with a few additions.

The Better Approach

Provide context, constraints, and voice:

> I need to email our vendor contact, Maria Chen at Apex Supply Co. We have a good relationship — we've been working together for four years. I need to push our Q2 order (PO-2026-0847) back by three weeks, from April 15 to May 6. The reason is a warehouse renovation that affects our receiving dock.
>
> Write the email in a warm but professional tone. Keep it under 150 words. I want to: 1. Acknowledge that this is a schedule change on our end 2. Clearly state the new delivery date 3. Ask if the revised timeline works on their end 4. Mention that I'm happy to discuss by phone if needed
>
> My name is Sarah, Director of Operations at Greenfield Manufacturing.

The result will be noticeably better — more specific, better toned, and closer to what you would actually send. The extra thirty seconds on the prompt saves you several minutes of editing.

Handling Difficult Emails

Difficult emails are where AI earns its keep. The message to an underperforming employee. The pushback on an unreasonable deadline. The response to a customer complaint. These are the emails you agonize over, draft and re-draft, and sometimes put off for hours.

Here is a prompt for a tough situation:

> I need to respond to a client email. The client, David Park at Meridian Financial, is upset because our Q1 deliverable was three days late. He's right to be frustrated — we missed the deadline because of an internal

> staffing issue that was our fault. However, the deliverable quality is excellent and I want to acknowledge the delay while redirecting to the strong work product.
>
> Context: Meridian is a $200K annual account. David tends to be direct and appreciates when people don't make excuses. Our relationship is strong but this is the second time we've been late this year.
>
> Write a response that: 1. Takes clear responsibility without being overly apologetic or groveling 2. Briefly explains what we're doing to prevent future delays (we're adding a dedicated project manager to their account) 3. Highlights key wins in the deliverable to shift focus forward 4. Keeps the tone confident and professional
>
> Maximum 200 words.

This prompt gives the AI enough context to produce something you would actually send. Without that context — "respond to an upset client" — you get something generic and possibly inappropriate for the relationship.

Email Triage and Summarization

Writing emails is only half the problem. The other half is dealing with the avalanche of incoming messages.

Summarizing Long Email Threads

One of AI's most immediately useful capabilities. Take a 15-message email thread, paste it into your AI tool, and ask:

> Summarize this email thread. Give me: 1. The key issue or topic 2. Each person's position 3. Current status — what has been decided vs. what is still open 4. Any action items with owners

What used to take ten minutes of scrolling and parsing takes thirty seconds. If you manage a team and regularly get added to threads already deep into discussion, this is a daily time-saver.

Prioritizing Your Inbox

If you process your email in batches — and you should — AI can help you triage. Copy your unread email subjects and senders into a prompt:

> Here are the 23 unread emails in my inbox. Categorize them by urgency:
>
> - URGENT: Requires response today
> - IMPORTANT: Needs response this week
> - FYI: Read when available
> - DELEGATE: Someone on my team should handle this
>
> [paste subject lines and senders]

Particularly useful for executives and managers who return from meetings to find their inbox has exploded.

Extracting Action Items

After receiving a long email or set of instructions:

> Extract all action items from this email. For each one, identify: - What needs to be done - Who is responsible (if specified) - The deadline (if mentioned) - Any dependencies

This works beautifully for post-meeting emails, project updates, and those long emails from your boss that contain seven requests buried in four paragraphs.

Adjusting Tone and Register

One of AI's most practical email capabilities is tone adjustment. You write what you mean; AI makes it sound the way it needs to sound.

When You Need to Sound More Diplomatic

Your instinct: "This proposal doesn't make sense and will waste everyone's time."

The prompt:

> Rewrite this sentence to be diplomatically professional while still expressing concern about feasibility: "This proposal doesn't make sense and will waste everyone's time."

AI output: "I appreciate the initiative behind this proposal, and I want to make sure we've fully considered the resource implications before moving forward. Could we schedule thirty minutes to walk through the feasibility analysis?"

When You Need to Be More Direct

The opposite problem: you have written a soft, hedging email and it needs more clarity.

> Make this email more direct and actionable. Remove hedging language (words like "maybe," "might," "perhaps," "I was wondering if"). Keep the professional tone but make the requests clear and specific.

When You Need to Match Someone's Style

> Here is an email from my CEO. Analyze her communication style — tone, sentence length, level of formality, how she structures requests. Then help me draft a reply that matches her communication preferences.

Surprisingly effective. AI picks up on patterns in writing style and can help you calibrate your communication to your audience.

Internal Communications

AI is equally useful for internal business communications: team announcements, policy updates, change communications, and all-hands messages.

Team Announcements

> Write an internal announcement to my team of 15 people. We're restructuring the project management function — moving from individual PM ownership to a pod-based model where three PMs will each lead a pod of cross-functional team members.
>
> I need to: - Explain the change clearly and simply - Acknowledge that change is uncomfortable - Explain why we're doing this (better cross-functional collaboration, more resilience when someone is out) - Note that no one is losing their job or getting demoted - Invite questions at our Thursday team meeting
>
> Tone: warm, confident, honest. Not corporate-speak.

Policy Communications

> I need to communicate our new AI usage policy to the entire company. The key points are:

1. We encourage AI tool use for productivity
2. Never put confidential client data into free-tier AI tools
3. All client-facing content generated with AI must be reviewed by a human
4. We're providing licenses for [tool] — see IT for access
5. We're not monitoring individual AI usage, but we expect responsible use

> Write this as an email from the COO. Professional but not stuffy. Under 300 words.

Slack and Teams Messages

Business communication increasingly happens in messaging platforms, not email. AI helps here too, though the approach differs slightly because messages tend to be shorter and more conversational.

Quick Response Drafting

For Slack-style messages, brevity matters more than formality. Tell AI this explicitly:

> Draft a short Slack message to the marketing team. We need all Q2 campaign briefs submitted by Friday COB. This is the second time I'm asking — some people missed the first deadline. Be firm but not harsh. Keep it under 50 words.

Summarizing Channel Activity

If you have been offline and need to catch up on a busy Slack channel:

> Here's the conversation from the #product-launch channel from today. Summarize what I missed and flag anything that needs my input or decision.

Templates and Reusable Prompts

One of the highest-leverage moves you can make is creating a library of email prompt templates for your recurring communication needs. A few to get you started:

The Meeting Follow-Up Template: > Write a follow-up email after a meeting. Meeting was with [person/group] about [topic]. Key decisions: [list]. Action items: [list with owners and deadlines]. Next meeting: [date]. Keep it concise and professional.

The Project Status Update Template: > Write a project status update email for [project name]. Include sections for: Completed This Week, In Progress, Upcoming, Risks/Blockers. Tone should be clear and factual. Here are the details: [paste your notes].

The Introduction Email Template: > Write a double opt-in introduction email connecting [Person A, title, company] with [Person B, title, company]. The reason for the connection is [reason]. Keep it brief and make it easy for both parties to take the next step.

The Thank-You-After-Interview Template: > Write a thank-you email to [interviewer name] at [company]. The role is [position]. We discussed [key topics]. I want to reinforce [specific strength] and express genuine enthusiasm without being over-the-top. Keep it under 150 words.

Best Practices for AI-Assisted Email

After watching hundreds of professionals integrate AI into their email workflow, here are the patterns that separate effective users from everyone else.

Always edit. Never send an AI-generated email without reviewing and personalizing it. Add a personal reference, adjust a phrase to match your voice, verify any facts. The draft saves you time; the edit makes it yours.

Provide context, not just instructions. The difference between "write a professional email declining a meeting" and "write an email to my colleague Jim declining his weekly sync — I'm overcommitted this quarter and need to protect my calendar, but I want to keep the door open for a monthly check-in" is the difference between a generic template and a useful draft.

Use AI for the emails you dread. The highest return on AI investment is in the emails you would otherwise procrastinate on — the difficult conversations, the uncomfortable feedback, the delicate negotiations. These are where AI's ability to find the right tone and structure is most valuable.

Build your voice profile. Give your AI tool a few examples of emails you have written and liked. Ask it to identify your writing style. Then reference that style in future prompts: "Write this in my style — direct, concise, occasionally dry humor, no exclamation points."

Batch your email AI work. Rather than opening an AI tool for each individual email, collect your email tasks and process them in a batch. Open your AI tool, draft five emails in a row, then switch to editing mode. Faster, and keeps you in flow.

What AI Cannot Do with Email

A few important limitations:

AI does not read your inbox. Unless you use an integrated tool like Copilot in Outlook or Gemini in Gmail, you need to manually copy email content into your AI tool. This adds friction but gives you control over what information you share.

AI does not understand office politics. It can write a diplomatically worded email, but it does not know that the recipient is your CEO's pet project champion and that the phrasing needs to account for that. You bring the organizational awareness.

AI occasionally gets tone wrong. An email AI thinks is "warm and professional" might read as sycophantic to you. What AI considers "direct" might come across as blunt. Always calibrate the output against your knowledge of the recipient.

AI does not know what you should say — only how to say it. The strategic decision about whether to accept the meeting, push back on the deadline, or raise the concern is yours. AI helps you express your decision effectively once you have made it.

The Time Savings Are Real

Here is what a typical professional sees after incorporating AI into their email workflow for a month:

- Time spent drafting emails: down 40 to 60 percent
- Time spent on email triage and summarization: down 30 to 50 percent
- Overall email processing time: down 30 to 40 percent
- Number of emails put off due to difficulty: down significantly

- Quality and consistency of email communication: up

For someone who spends two hours a day on email, that is roughly 40 to 50 minutes of recovered time — every single day. Over a year, more than 170 hours.

That is four full work weeks. Just from email.

Chapter 5: Meetings and Collaboration

The average professional spends somewhere between 20 and 30 hours a month in meetings — and managers spend considerably more. That is a meaningful chunk of any work week sitting in conference rooms or staring at video calls, and it does not count the prep, the write-ups, or the action items that somehow evaporate the moment everyone leaves the room.

AI cannot eliminate meetings — and you probably would not want it to, since well-run meetings are where decisions get made and teams align. But AI can dramatically reduce the overhead around them: the prep time, the note-taking, the follow-up, and the administrative friction that turns a thirty-minute meeting into a ninety-minute productivity black hole.

Before the Meeting: Preparation

Meeting preparation is one of the highest-ROI applications of AI in business. Most people either over-prepare (hours building decks nobody needs) or under-prepare (winging it and wasting everyone's time). AI lets you do the right amount of homework in a fraction of the time.

Building an Agenda

A well-structured agenda is the single biggest predictor of a productive meeting. Most people know this. Most still do not write one. AI makes it easy.

> I'm leading a 45-minute meeting with the marketing team (6 people) to review our Q2 content strategy. We need to cover: - Performance of Q1 content (blog traffic, social engagement, lead gen) - Proposed themes for Q2 - Budget allocation across channels - Timeline for the product launch campaign (launching May 15)
>
> Create a timed agenda that keeps us on track. Include time for discussion on contentious items (budget is usually where we get stuck). Reserve 5 minutes at the end for action items and next steps.

You get a structured, realistic agenda with time allocations. Adjust the times based on which topics you know will generate the most discussion, and you have a meeting plan in under two minutes.

Pre-Meeting Research and Briefing

If you are meeting with someone external — a prospective client, a vendor, a partner — AI can help you prepare a quick briefing.

> I have a meeting tomorrow with Sarah Kim, VP of Marketing at Ridgeline Health. We've never met. Help me prepare:
>
> 1. What should I know about Ridgeline Health? (They're a mid-size healthcare tech company based in Austin.)
> 2. What is their likely marketing stack and challenges given their industry and size?
> 3. What questions should I ask to understand their needs?
> 4. Any recent news about the company I should be aware of?

For current information, run this through Perplexity, which searches the web in real time. For general prep and question generation, any AI tool will do.

Preparing Talking Points

When you are presenting in a meeting rather than leading it:

> I'm presenting a proposal to add two headcount to the customer success team. My audience is the CFO and VP of Operations. They care about ROI and are skeptical of headcount increases.
>
> My key data points: - Customer churn increased 12% last quarter - Each churned enterprise customer = $85K ARR lost - We lost 7 enterprise customers last quarter ($595K) - Two senior CS reps would cost approximately $180K total (loaded) - Industry benchmark is 1 CS rep per 30 accounts; we're at 1:52
>
> Help me structure a 5-minute pitch with clear talking points that lead with the financial argument.

AI excels at structuring arguments and anticipating objections — exactly what you need before walking into a room where you have to win approval.

Reviewing Previous Meeting Notes

If you have notes from the last meeting on the same topic, feed them to the AI:

> Here are the notes from our last product steering committee meeting (March 5). I have another meeting with the same group on March 19. Help me: 1. Identify open action items from the last meeting 2. Flag decisions that were deferred 3. Suggest topics we should address at the upcoming meeting based on what was discussed

A simple way to keep continuity between meetings — something that usually gets lost because nobody reads last meeting's notes.

During the Meeting: Note-Taking

Real-time AI meeting assistance has become one of the fastest-growing categories of business AI in 2025 and 2026. The proposition is simple: the AI joins your meeting, records the audio, transcribes it, and produces structured notes.

Dedicated Meeting AI Tools

Several tools specialize in this:

- **Otter.ai** provides real-time transcription with speaker identification, searchable transcripts, and AI-generated summaries
- **Fireflies.ai** records, transcribes, and creates meeting summaries with action items
- **Microsoft Copilot in Teams** does this natively for Teams meetings if your organization has Copilot licenses
- **Google Gemini in Meet** provides similar capabilities for Google Meet users

These tools have become genuinely good. Speaker identification is accurate most of the time. Transcription quality is high. The summaries capture the substance of the conversation with impressive fidelity.

How to Use Meeting AI Effectively

A few practical tips from organizations that have adopted meeting AI successfully:

Tell participants. This should go without saying, but always inform attendees that the meeting is being recorded and transcribed. Most tools add a visible bot to the call, but verbal confirmation is both courteous and — in many jurisdictions — legally required.

Review and edit the summary. AI meeting summaries are good but not perfect. They miss nuance, misattribute statements, or overlook important context. Spend five minutes reviewing before distributing.

Use the transcript for specifics. The summary captures the highlights. The full transcript is your backup when you need to verify exactly what someone said or find a detail the summary missed.

Do not let meeting AI make you lazy about preparation. Knowing everything will be captured does not mean you should show up unprepared. If anything, better meeting records raise accountability.

When You Cannot Use Meeting AI

Some meetings should not be recorded: sensitive HR discussions, confidential strategy sessions, early-stage negotiations, anything involving legal privilege. For these meetings, take manual notes and use AI after the fact.

> Here are my handwritten notes from today's board meeting (I've typed them up quickly, they're rough). Clean them up into a structured summary with: - Key decisions made - Action items with owners - Open questions - Items tabled for next meeting

Scattered bullets and rough shorthand become meeting minutes in thirty seconds.

After the Meeting: Follow-Up

Post-meeting follow-up is where meetings either produce results or fade into the "that was a waste of time" pile. AI makes good follow-up nearly effortless.

The Follow-Up Email

> Based on this meeting summary, write a follow-up email to all attendees. Include: 1. Brief recap of key decisions (2-3 sentences max) 2. Action items table: who owns what, by when 3. Date of next meeting 4. Any materials or pre-work needed before next meeting

> Keep it concise — nobody wants a novel in their inbox after a meeting they just attended.

Action Item Tracking

One of the most consistently useful applications of AI in the meeting lifecycle:

> Here are the notes from our last three team meetings. Extract all action items and create a consolidated tracker showing: - Action item - Owner - Original due date - Status (overdue, due this week, upcoming) - Which meeting it was assigned in

This is the kind of administrative work nobody wants to do manually but that makes a real difference in team accountability.

Meeting-to-Document Conversion

Sometimes a meeting generates content that needs to be formalized. AI bridges that gap:

> In today's product planning meeting, we discussed and agreed on the feature priorities for the Q3 release. Here are the meeting notes. Convert them into a formal product requirements document that includes: - Feature name and description - Priority (P1/P2/P3) - Estimated effort - Dependencies - Success criteria

What would normally take an hour of post-meeting writing now happens in minutes.

Collaborative Work with AI

Beyond meetings specifically, AI enhances team collaboration in several ways.

Collaborative Document Drafting

When multiple people need to contribute to a document, AI can help coordinate:

> We're building a quarterly business review deck. I need to send a brief to each department head asking for their section. Create a template brief that includes: - What they need to submit (key metrics, narrative

> summary, challenges, plans) - Format specifications - Word/slide count limits - Deadline - Examples of what “good” looks like for their section
>
> Customize it for: Sales, Marketing, Product, Engineering, Customer Success, Finance.

Synthesizing Input from Multiple People

When you have received input from several team members:

> I received input from six department heads for our QBR. Here are all six submissions. Synthesize them into a coherent executive summary that: - Highlights the top 3 cross-functional themes - Identifies areas of alignment and disagreement - Calls out the 3 most significant risks mentioned across departments - Summarizes the overall health of the business in 2-3 sentences

This kind of synthesis — pulling common threads from disparate inputs — is something AI does remarkably well and that humans find tedious and slow.

Brainstorming and Ideation

AI can serve as a brainstorming partner for team activities:

> Our team is brainstorming solutions to our customer onboarding problem. New customers take an average of 45 days to fully onboard, and our target is 21 days. The main bottlenecks are: data migration (slow, manual), user training (scheduled weeks out), and IT provisioning (requires too many approvals).
>
> Generate 15 ideas for reducing onboarding time. Include a mix of: - Quick fixes we could implement this quarter - Medium-term process improvements - Bold ideas that would require investment but could be transformative
>
> For each idea, estimate the potential time reduction.

Use this as the starting point for a team brainstorm. It primes the conversation, which beats starting with a blank whiteboard and waiting for someone to speak first.

Managing Meeting Overload

AI can also help with the meta-problem: too many meetings in the first place.

Meeting Audit

> Here is my calendar for the last two weeks. I had [X] meetings. For each recurring meeting, help me evaluate: - Is this meeting still necessary? - Could it be an email or async update instead? - Is the frequency right, or could we meet less often? - Am I the right person to attend, or could I delegate? - Is the meeting the right length?
>
> Be ruthless. My goal is to recover at least 5 hours per week.

The Async Alternative

For meetings that could be asynchronous:

> Instead of our weekly 30-minute marketing sync, I want to try an async format. Design a weekly async update template that each team member fills out by Monday at noon. It should capture everything we'd normally discuss in the meeting but take less than 10 minutes to complete.

Building a Meeting Culture with AI

If you are a manager or team lead, you can set norms around AI-enhanced meetings. Practices I have seen work well:

Every meeting gets an AI-generated agenda. Make agenda creation a habit, not an exception. Two minutes, dramatically better meetings.

Share AI summaries within two hours. If you are using meeting transcription, distribute the summary same-day while the conversation is still fresh. It becomes the single source of truth.

Track action items in one place. Whether in a project management tool or a shared document, use AI to extract action items from every meeting and feed them into a central tracker. Review open items at the start of each subsequent meeting.

Default to shorter meetings. With AI handling prep and follow-up, meetings can focus on discussion and decisions. Most sixty-minute meetings can hit the same goals in thirty when the prep and follow-up happen outside the meeting with AI.

Cancel meetings that do not need to happen. Use the async alternative whenever the primary purpose is information sharing rather than discussion or decisions.

The Compound Effect

The real power of AI in meetings is not any single application — it is the compound effect across the entire lifecycle.

Before the meeting: five minutes of AI-assisted prep instead of thirty. During the meeting: AI captures everything so you can focus on the conversation. After the meeting: five minutes editing an AI-generated summary instead of twenty writing notes from scratch. Action items captured automatically.

Each improvement is modest on its own. Together, they turn meetings from a productivity drain into a well-oiled machine. For most professionals, the total time saved on meeting-related overhead is five to eight hours per week.

That is not a marginal improvement. That is a structural change in how you spend your time.

Chapter 6: Reports and Documents

Every business runs on documents. Quarterly reports. Board decks. Project proposals. Strategic plans. Executive summaries. Client deliverables. Internal briefs. Policy documents. SOWs and SOPs and RFPs and all the other acronyms that fill your professional life.

The dirty secret of business documents is that most follow predictable structures, contain similar information, and serve broadly similar purposes. That makes them ideal candidates for AI. Not because AI can write your documents without your input — it cannot, at least not well — but because it accelerates every phase of the process: planning, drafting, structuring, editing, polishing.

The Document Creation Workflow

Most business documents follow a four-phase workflow. AI helps at every phase.

Phase 1: Planning and Structure

Before writing a word, you need to know what you are writing and how to organize it. This is where many people get stuck — not for lack of information, but because they are unsure how to structure it.

> I need to write a proposal for a $150K technology infrastructure upgrade for our company (85 employees, B2B SaaS). The audience is our CEO and CFO. They will use this to decide whether to approve the capital expenditure.
>
> Help me plan the document structure. What sections should I include, in what order, and what should each section accomplish? Keep in mind that the CFO cares primarily about cost justification and ROI, while the CEO cares about competitive advantage and risk.

AI produces a logical outline tailored to your audience. You adjust it based on what you know will resonate with these specific decision-makers, and you have a roadmap in under two minutes.

Phase 2: First Draft

This is where AI delivers the most dramatic time savings. Instead of staring at a blank screen, you feed AI your outline, data, and key messages, and it produces a complete first draft.

> Write the "Executive Summary" section of this proposal. Key points to cover:
>
> - Our current infrastructure is 6 years old and reaching end of life
> - We experienced 14 unplanned outages last year, totaling 87 hours of downtime
> - Each hour of downtime costs approximately $4,200 in lost productivity and revenue
> - Total cost of downtime last year: ~$365K
> - Proposed upgrade cost: $150K (one-time) + $12K/year in incremental maintenance
> - Expected outcome: reduce unplanned downtime by 85% and support our planned growth from 85 to 130 employees over the next 3 years
>
> Make it persuasive but not salesy. These are internal decision-makers who appreciate straightforward analysis.

Work the document section by section, feeding AI the key information and getting polished prose back. For a ten-page proposal, this cuts drafting time from a full day to an hour.

Phase 3: Review and Refinement

Once you have a draft, AI becomes an editor and a critic.

> Review this draft proposal for the infrastructure upgrade. Check for: 1. Logical gaps — are there claims that aren't supported by data? 2. Tone consistency — does it maintain a professional, analytical voice throughout? 3. Persuasiveness — would a skeptical CFO find this compelling? 4. Conciseness — identify paragraphs that could be tightened 5. Missing elements — is anything important left out?

A second pair of eyes before the document reaches your colleagues. AI's feedback does not replace human review — you still want a colleague reading important documents before they go to leadership — but it catches the issues you are too close to the document to see.

Phase 4: Polish

The final pass addresses presentation quality.

> Polish this document for submission. Specifically: - Ensure consistent formatting (headings, bullet styles, number formats) - Check for jargon that the CFO might not know and either explain it or replace it - Verify that all numbers in the text match the numbers in the tables - Improve transitions between sections - Write a strong closing paragraph that clearly states the ask

Common Business Documents

A walk through AI approaches for the documents you are most likely to create.

Executive Summaries

The executive summary is probably the document type where AI delivers the most outsized value. Executives are busy. They need the bottom line fast.

> Summarize this 25-page quarterly business review into a 1-page executive summary. Structure it as:

- **Bottom line** (2-3 sentences): How are we doing?
- **Key wins** (3-4 bullet points): What went well?
- **Key concerns** (2-3 bullet points): What needs attention?
- **Key numbers** (table): Revenue, margin, customer count, NPS — actual vs. target
- **Outlook** (2-3 sentences): What to expect next quarter

> Write for a board audience. Be direct. No fluff.

Compressing a long document into a tight summary without losing the essentials is one of AI's strongest capabilities.

Project Proposals

Write a project proposal for implementing a customer feedback system. Include:

- Problem statement: We currently have no systematic way to collect and act on customer feedback. Feedback comes through random channels — sales calls, support tickets, occasional surveys — and is never aggregated.
- Proposed solution: Implement a structured feedback program using [tool] with quarterly surveys, post-interaction feedback, and a centralized dashboard
- Timeline: 8 weeks from approval to launch
- Budget: $35K first year ($15K implementation + $20K annual license)
- Expected outcomes: Baseline NPS within 3 months, 10-point NPS improvement within 12 months, reduction in churn by identifying at-risk accounts earlier
- Risks: Low adoption if not mandated; survey fatigue if over-deployed
- Team: Requires 0.25 FTE from CS, 0.1 FTE from Engineering for integration

Audience: VP of Customer Success and CFO.

Status Reports

Create a weekly project status report for the CRM migration project. Format it as:

Project: CRM Migration (Salesforce to HubSpot) **Week ending:** March 28, 2026 **Overall status:** [choose Yellow]

Here are my rough notes from this week: - Data migration phase 2 finished on time, 45K contacts moved - Found duplicate records in the legacy system, about 8K dupes, need to resolve before go-live - Training sessions started, 3 of 7 completed - Integration with Zendesk hitting API rate limits, eng working on it - Go-live still targeted for April 21 but at risk if API issue isn't resolved by April 7

Turn this into a professional status report with RAG ratings for each workstream.

Business Cases

> Write a business case for hiring a dedicated data analyst. Our company (200 employees, B2B software) currently has no one whose primary job is data analysis. Instead, analysis is done ad hoc by marketing, sales, and product managers who are not trained analysts.
>
> Arguments for: - We're making $2M in marketing spend decisions annually based on gut feeling and basic spreadsheets - Product prioritization meetings frequently devolve into opinion wars because no one has done the analysis - Sales cannot accurately forecast because pipeline data is messy - Competitors our size typically have 1-3 dedicated analysts
>
> Cost: approximately $95K total comp + $15K in tools (Looker/Tableau license, etc.)
>
> Build the business case with a clear ROI argument.

Standard Operating Procedures

SOPs are tedious to write from scratch, but they follow predictable structures AI handles well.

> Write a standard operating procedure for our customer onboarding process. Here are the steps as I know them (rough):
>
> 1. Sales closes deal, sends intro email to CS
> 2. CS manager assigns account to CS rep within 24 hours
> 3. CS rep sends welcome email with scheduling link
> 4. Kickoff call within first week — agenda includes intro, goals, timeline, access setup
> 5. Technical setup — CS rep works with client IT for SSO, data import
> 6. Training — 3 sessions over 2 weeks
> 7. Go-live check — CS rep verifies everything works
> 8. 30-day check-in
> 9. Transfer to ongoing support
>
> Format each step with: responsible party, timeline, inputs needed, outputs produced, escalation path if delayed. Make it a real SOP that a new hire could follow on day one.

Working with Long Documents

One of AI's most practical business applications is processing long documents — work that used to be pure manual labor.

Summarizing Documents

> I'm uploading our company's 40-page employee handbook. I need you to: 1. Create a 2-page summary of the key policies every employee should know 2. Flag any policies that seem outdated or conflict with each other 3. Identify any topics that are missing (common handbook sections we don't have)

Comparing Documents

> I'm uploading two versions of our vendor contract — the version from last year and the version our vendor just sent for renewal. Compare them and identify: - Every change, no matter how small - Changes that affect our financial obligations - Changes to service level agreements - New clauses that weren't in the original - Anything that should concern us or that we should negotiate

Extracting Information

> This 60-page RFP from a potential client contains requirements scattered throughout the document. Extract every requirement and organize them into a table with columns for: requirement number, requirement description, category (technical/business/compliance), and whether we can meet it (leave this blank for me to fill in).

Document Quality Checklist

Before finalizing any important business document, run it through this AI quality check:

> Review this document against this checklist:

1. **Clarity:** Is every sentence unambiguous? Flag any passages that could be interpreted multiple ways.
2. **Completeness:** Are there claims without evidence or questions raised without answers?

3. **Consistency:** Do numbers, terminology, and formatting remain consistent throughout?
4. **Audience fit:** Is the language appropriate for the intended reader? Flag jargon, overly technical passages, or insufficient detail.
5. **Action orientation:** Is it clear what the reader should do after reading this? Is the ask explicit?
6. **Conciseness:** Flag redundant sections, unnecessary qualifiers, and passages that could be shortened without losing meaning.

> For each issue found, suggest a specific fix.

Adapting Documents for Different Audiences

A powerful, underused AI capability: taking one document and adapting it for different readers.

> I've written a detailed technical assessment of our cybersecurity posture. I need to create three versions:
>
> 1. **Board version** (1 page): Risk-focused, business impact language, no technical jargon, clear recommendations with cost implications
> 2. **Executive team version** (3 pages): Moderate technical detail, emphasis on operational impact and resource needs, prioritized action items
> 3. **IT team version** (keep the full technical detail but add an implementation priority matrix)
>
> Here is the original document. Create all three versions.

Multi-audience adaptation that would normally take hours. AI does it in minutes, and the results are usually solid because the core information stays consistent while framing and detail level shift to fit each reader.

Templates for Recurring Documents

If you create the same type of document regularly — monthly reports, quarterly reviews, project charters — build a template once and reuse it.

> I need to create a template for our monthly marketing report. Every month, I'll fill in the data and AI will generate the narrative. Design the template with:

- Placeholder fields for the data I'll provide each month (traffic, leads, conversion rates, campaign performance, budget vs. actual)
- Standard sections that the narrative should follow
- Tone guidelines (professional, data-driven, concise)
- A prompt template I can reuse each month by just swapping in the numbers

Once the template exists, your monthly report goes from a four-hour exercise to a thirty-minute task.

The Editing Pass: Making AI Output Sound Like You

AI-generated business documents have a recognizable quality when left unedited. Well-structured but slightly generic, correct but not distinctive, professional but lacking personality.

The editing pass is where you turn competent AI output into something that sounds like you and your organization. Focus on:

Remove AI-isms. Watch for phrases like "in today's rapidly evolving business landscape," "leverage synergies," "it's important to note that," and "in conclusion." These are AI comfort phrases — they fill space without meaning.

Add your voice. If you are known for being direct, cut the hedging. If your culture uses specific terminology, swap it in. If an inside reference would resonate with your audience, add it.

Inject specifics. AI writes in generalizations unless you give it specifics. Replace "improved significantly" with "improved 23% quarter over quarter." Replace "a major client" with the actual name (when appropriate for the audience).

Verify everything. Check every number, every claim, every recommendation. AI is good at structure and prose, but it sometimes introduces plausible-sounding details that are fabricated. If a number appears in the output that was not in your input, verify it or remove it.

The Bottom Line

Business documents are the medium through which decisions get made, resources get allocated, and work gets done. AI does not change that — it just means you spend less time wrestling with structure and prose and more time on the thinking and analysis that make documents valuable.

The professional who used to spend Friday afternoon grinding out a status report now spends thirty minutes reviewing an AI-generated draft. The manager who dreaded the quarterly business review produces a polished document in a quarter of the time. The analyst who procrastinated on the annual strategy brief has a structured first draft before lunch.

Better documents, less time. That is the promise, and in 2026, it consistently delivers.

Chapter 7: Presentations

Presentations occupy a unique position in business. They are simultaneously one of the most high-stakes and most time-consuming tasks professionals face. A good presentation can win a deal, secure funding, align a team, or convince the board. A bad one wastes everyone's time and damages your credibility.

The problem is that building a good presentation takes a lot of time. A serious deck for a high-stakes meeting can easily eat the better part of a workday — and that is just preparation, not counting rehearsal. Much of that time goes into tasks AI handles well: organizing content, writing slide copy, creating talking points, structuring the narrative arc.

Let me be clear about what AI can and cannot do here. AI is excellent at helping you think through your story, structure your slides, and write the text on them. It is getting better at visual design, but it is not yet a replacement for a skilled designer on high-stakes work. Think of AI as a presentation strategist and copywriter, not a graphic designer.

Planning Your Presentation

Every good presentation starts with the same three questions: What is the goal? Who is the audience? What do they need to hear?

AI helps you think through these more rigorously than you might on your own.

> I need to prepare a 20-minute presentation for our company's leadership team (CEO, CFO, CTO, VP of Sales, VP of Marketing). The purpose is to get approval and budget for a new customer data platform.
>
> Help me plan this presentation: 1. What is the core argument I need to make? 2. What are the likely objections from each stakeholder given their role? 3. What data or evidence would be most compelling? 4. What is the ideal narrative arc for a 20-minute pitch to this audience? 5. How many slides should I target, and what should each one accomplish?

This is the step most people skip and regret later. Five minutes thinking through audience and narrative with AI prevents the common mistake of building slides organized around your logic rather than your audience's concerns.

Building the Slide Outline

Once you have a plan, AI can create a detailed slide-by-slide outline.

> Based on our planning discussion, create a slide-by-slide outline for this presentation. For each slide, include: - Slide title - Key message (the one thing the audience should take away from this slide) - Content notes (what data, examples, or visuals should appear) - Speaker notes (what I should say that is NOT on the slide)
>
> Target 15 slides for a 20-minute presentation. Include an executive summary slide at the beginning and a clear "ask" slide at the end.

One of the most useful prompts in this entire book. The output is a complete blueprint for your presentation. Hand this outline to anyone — a colleague, a designer, or yourself at 9 PM the night before — and they have everything they need to build the deck.

Writing Slide Content

With the outline in hand, AI helps you write the slide content. The key principle for slide text is less is more. Slides are visual aids for your spoken words, not documents to be read aloud.

> Write the slide content for slides 3 through 7 of my presentation outline. Follow these rules: - Maximum 6 lines of text per slide - Maximum 8 words per line - Use sentence fragments, not complete sentences - Lead with the insight, not the data - Every slide should have a clear "so what" that connects to our ask

For data-heavy slides:

> Write the content for my "Current State" slide. The data points are: - Customer data spread across 7 disconnected systems - 34% of customer records have at least one data quality issue - Sales team spends average 45 minutes per day searching for customer information - Marketing campaigns targeting the wrong segments 23% of the time due to bad data

> Structure this as a visual slide — suggest whether to use a chart, a comparison table, an icon grid, or another visual format. Write the headline and supporting text.

Talking Points and Speaker Notes

The best presenters know that what you say matters more than what is on the slide. AI helps you prepare the spoken component.

> For each slide in my presentation, write speaker notes that: - Expand on the slide content without simply reading the slide aloud - Include a transition sentence to the next slide - Note where I should pause for questions or reactions - Suggest where to use a specific example or anecdote - Keep each slide's speaking time to approximately 90 seconds

Anticipating Questions

> Based on this presentation, what questions is each member of my audience likely to ask? For each anticipated question, draft a concise answer.
>
> Be especially thorough about: - CFO questions (cost, ROI, alternatives considered) - CTO questions (technical architecture, integration complexity, vendor lock-in) - CEO questions (strategic alignment, competitive implications, timeline)

This is the prep that separates confident presenters from nervous ones. When someone asks a tough question and you have a clear, thoughtful answer ready, your credibility jumps.

AI-Powered Presentation Tools

Several tools now generate complete slide decks from prompts or documents.

Gamma

Gamma has emerged as the leading AI-native presentation tool. Describe what you want, and it generates a complete, designed presentation with layout, images, and formatting. The results are surprisingly polished for a first draft.

Best for: Quick internal presentations, team updates, and cases where design quality matters but no designer is available.

Limitations: Designs can feel templated, and complex data visualizations need manual adjustment.

Beautiful.ai

Beautiful.ai uses AI to handle design decisions — layout, alignment, spacing, color — as you build slides. You focus on content; it handles aesthetics.

Best for: Professionals who want more control over content than Gamma offers but less design friction than PowerPoint.

Microsoft Copilot in PowerPoint

If you are in the Microsoft ecosystem, Copilot can generate slides from a prompt, convert a Word document into a presentation, and redesign existing slides.

Best for: Teams already on Microsoft 365 who want to stay within familiar tools.

Limitations: Generated slides often need significant refinement, and the design capabilities are still catching up to dedicated tools.

Google Gemini in Slides

Gemini helps with content generation and image creation inside Google Slides, though it is less capable at full deck generation than dedicated tools.

Best for: Teams on Google Workspace who want AI assistance without leaving their primary tool.

Using ChatGPT or Claude for Presentations

The general-purpose AI tools do not generate slide decks directly, but they are often the best tools for the thinking and writing parts. Use them for planning, outlining, writing content, and preparing speaking notes, then transfer the output into your presentation tool of choice.

My recommended workflow:

1. Plan and outline in Claude or ChatGPT (best thinking and writing)

2. Generate the visual deck in Gamma or Beautiful.ai (best design)
3. Refine in PowerPoint or Google Slides (most control)

Presentation Types and Approaches

Different presentations have different requirements. AI approaches for the most common types:

The Sales Pitch

> Help me build a sales presentation for [prospect company]. Our product is [description]. The prospect's key challenge is [challenge]. They are currently using [competitor/current solution].
>
> Structure the deck as: 1. Their problem (make it specific to them) 2. Why current solutions fall short 3. Our approach (not features — outcomes) 4. Proof (case studies, metrics from similar customers) 5. What working with us looks like 6. Investment and next steps
>
> Tone: consultative, not salesy. They should feel understood, not pitched.

The Board Presentation

> I'm presenting to the board of directors. The presentation covers our Q1 results and Q2 outlook. Board members have limited time and want the bottom line fast.
>
> Rules for board presentations: - Lead with the conclusion, then support it - Use consistent RAG (Red/Amber/Green) status indicators - Limit text — use charts and visuals instead - Every slide must answer "so what?" and "what do we need from the board?" - Include an appendix with detailed data for those who want to dig in

The Team All-Hands

> Build a slide outline for our monthly all-hands meeting (45 minutes, 60 people). Topics: - Company performance snapshot - Major wins from last month (recognize specific people and teams) - Key priorities for the coming month - Product update - New hire introductions - Open Q&A
>
> Keep it energetic and concise. This audience has heard too many boring all-hands meetings.

The Training Presentation

> I need to build a training deck for our new customer onboarding process. Audience: 12 customer success managers with varying experience levels. Duration: 90 minutes including exercises.
>
> Design the deck to be interactive — include places for group discussion, exercises, and hands-on practice. Break it into modules that can also be used independently for future reference.

Improving Existing Presentations

AI is just as useful for upgrading presentations you have already built.

Tightening Verbose Slides

> Here are my slides (I've pasted the text from each one). They're too wordy. For each slide, reduce the text by at least 50% while preserving the key message. Tell me what to cut and what to move to speaker notes.

Strengthening the Narrative

> Review this presentation outline and assess the narrative flow. Does each slide logically lead to the next? Is there a clear buildup to the ask? Identify any slides that are out of order, redundant, or missing.

Adding Impact

> These slides are factually solid but flat. For each slide, suggest one way to make it more impactful — a compelling statistic, a vivid analogy, a provocative question, or a visual element that would drive the point home.

The Visual Element

AI text generation for presentations is mature. AI-generated visuals are still evolving. Where things stand:

AI-generated images (via ChatGPT's DALL-E, Midjourney, or similar) can create custom illustrations, concept visuals, and background images. Quality varies, and you have to be specific about what you want. They work well for conceptual illustrations ("create an image representing data silos in an organization") but poorly for precise business graphics.

AI-generated charts and graphs are best built in tools designed for data visualization. Upload your data to ChatGPT or Claude, ask for a chart, then refine in Excel or a dedicated tool.

Stock photo alternatives. Instead of generic stock photos, use AI to generate custom images that fit your specific narrative. "A diverse team collaborating in a modern office" from an AI image generator will be more relevant than a stock photo that has appeared in a thousand other decks.

Rehearsal and Delivery

AI can even help you prepare to deliver the presentation.

> I've completed my presentation. Help me prepare for delivery: 1. Time check: given the speaker notes, estimate how long each section will take. Flag if I'm over my 20-minute target. 2. Key phrases: for each slide, give me one memorable phrase or statement I should emphasize 3. Transitions: write smooth transition sentences between sections 4. Opening hook: give me 3 options for opening the presentation in a way that immediately engages the audience 5. Closing statement: write a strong closing that reinforces the key message and makes the ask unmistakable

Common Presentation Mistakes AI Helps You Avoid

Too many slides. AI-generated outlines tend to be more disciplined than the kitchen-sink approach most people take when building slides organically.

Slides that are documents. AI helps you separate what belongs on the slide from what belongs in speaker notes.

No clear story. AI is good at narrative structure. Let it help you find your through-line.

Weak closing. AI consistently produces stronger closing slides than most humans write, because it treats the closing as the culmination of a narrative rather than an afterthought.

No backup for tough questions. AI helps you anticipate and prepare for every question your audience might ask.

The Bottom Line

Presentations are a synthesis of thinking, writing, design, and performance. AI will not make you a great presenter — that takes practice, confidence, and the ability to read a room. But it dramatically reduces the time you spend building slides and preparing content, so you can focus on delivery.

The professional who used to spend eight hours building a major presentation now spends three, with a better-structured result. That is not incremental. That is a fundamentally different relationship with one of business's most demanding tasks.

Part III: Analysis and Research

"Without data, you are just another person with an opinion."

— W. Edwards Deming

Chapter 8: Data Analysis for Business

A truth about modern business: most organizations are drowning in data and starving for insight. Spreadsheets full of numbers, dashboards full of charts, databases full of records — and still, most important decisions are made on gut feel because nobody has time to dig through the data and figure out what it means.

AI changes that equation. Not because it turns you into a data scientist — it does not — but because it lets you ask questions of your data in plain English and get answers that previously required SQL, statistical training, or hours of manual spreadsheet work.

This chapter is for business professionals who work with data regularly but lack a technical analytics background. If you can open a spreadsheet and understand what a row and column are, you have enough to use everything in this chapter.

What AI Can Do with Your Data

Set realistic expectations before diving in.

AI can analyze structured data. Upload a spreadsheet or CSV to ChatGPT, Claude, or Gemini, and it can read the file, understand the structure, and answer questions. This works for sales data, financial reports, customer lists, survey results, marketing metrics, and any other tabular data.

AI can create visualizations. Ask for a chart, and most AI tools will generate one — bar, line, scatter, pie, heat maps. The visualizations are functional rather than beautiful, but they communicate the insight, which is what matters.

AI can identify patterns. "What trends do you see in this data?" is a genuinely useful prompt. AI often surfaces patterns you would not have noticed because you were not looking for them.

AI can perform calculations. Averages, medians, growth rates, percentages, correlations, year-over-year comparisons — AI handles these accurately and explains the results in context.

AI cannot guarantee perfect accuracy. The critical caveat. AI occasionally makes calculation errors, misinterprets column headers, or draws conclusions the data does not support. Always verify important numbers. Treat AI as a very fast first-pass analyst whose work you review before relying on it.

Getting Started: Uploading Your Data

The mechanics of AI data analysis are straightforward. Most platforms support file uploads. What works:

Best formats: CSV works most reliably across all platforms. Excel files (.xlsx) are well-supported by ChatGPT and Claude. Google Sheets can be analyzed directly by Gemini.

Size limits: Limits vary by platform and tier and have moved upward steadily — check the current numbers before assuming. As a rule of thumb, files in the tens of megabytes work comfortably across major platforms, larger files work on most paid tiers, and anything beyond that is worth aggregating or sampling before uploading.

Data preparation: Before uploading, make sure your data has clear column headers, consistent formatting, and no merged cells. AI interprets data much better when it is clean and well-structured.

Privacy warning: Before uploading any data, confirm you are on a tier that does not train on your data (see Chapter 21). Never upload personally identifiable customer information to a free-tier AI tool.

The Five Questions Framework

When you have data and are not sure where to start, use these five questions. They work for virtually any business dataset.

Question 1: "What does this data tell us?"

Start broad and let the AI survey the landscape.

> I've uploaded our Q1 sales data. Give me an overview: - Total revenue and how it compares to Q1 last year - Top 10 customers by revenue -

> Revenue breakdown by product line - Average deal size - Any notable trends or anomalies

The initial scan often surfaces things you were not looking for — a product line growing faster than expected, a customer concentration risk, a seasonal pattern you had not noticed.

Question 2: "What changed?"

Most business analysis is about understanding change over time.

> Compare our Q1 2026 data to Q1 2025. Identify: - Which product lines grew and which declined? - Which customer segments changed most? - Are deal sizes trending larger or smaller? - How did our win rate change? - Were there any new customer segments we didn't have last year?

Question 3: "What are the patterns?"

AI excels at pattern recognition across large datasets.

> Analyze our customer churn data for the past 12 months. Look for patterns: - Are certain customer segments churning more than others? - Is there a common timeline — do customers tend to churn at specific points in their lifecycle? - Are churning customers concentrated in certain regions, industries, or product tiers? - Is there a correlation between customer engagement metrics and churn?

Question 4: "What should we worry about?"

Ask AI to play the role of a risk analyst.

> Based on this financial data, what should concern us? Look for: - Margins declining in specific areas - Revenue concentration risks - Expense growth outpacing revenue growth - Cash flow patterns that could become problematic - Any metric that is moving in the wrong direction

Question 5: "What should we do?"

This is where analysis becomes actionable.

Based on your analysis of our customer data, what are your top 5 recommendations? For each one: - What is the specific action? - What data supports this recommendation? - What is the expected impact? - How hard is it to implement?

Practical Data Analysis Scenarios

Sales Data Analysis

I've uploaded 12 months of sales data with columns: date, salesperson, account name, industry, deal value, product, stage, days in pipeline, won/lost.

Analyze this and answer: 1. What is our average sales cycle length? Has it changed over the year? 2. Which salesperson has the highest win rate? Which has the highest average deal size? 3. Are there industries where we win disproportionately? Where we lose? 4. What is the ideal deal size range — where is our win rate highest? 5. Create a chart showing pipeline velocity by quarter.

Marketing Performance Analysis

This spreadsheet contains our marketing campaign performance for the last 6 months. Columns: campaign name, channel, spend, impressions, clicks, conversions, revenue attributed.

I need to understand: 1. Cost per acquisition (CPA) by channel — which channels are most efficient? 2. Return on ad spend (ROAS) by campaign — which campaigns are actually profitable? 3. How does performance trend over time — are we getting better or worse? 4. If I had to cut 20% of our budget, which campaigns should I cut? Why? 5. Create a visualization showing CPA vs. volume by channel.

Financial Analysis

I've uploaded our P&L statement for the past 8 quarters. Analyze the trends and help me prepare for a budget discussion:

1. Revenue growth rate by quarter — is it accelerating or decelerating?
2. Which expense categories are growing fastest relative to revenue?
3. How has our gross margin trended? Operating margin?
4. If revenue grows at the current rate, when do we hit $10M ARR?

5. Create a waterfall chart showing the quarter-over-quarter changes in operating income.

Customer Analysis

> This dataset contains information on all our 850 customers: signup date, plan type, monthly spend, number of users, industry, region, health score, NPS score, last login date.
>
> Help me segment our customer base: 1. Create a simple segmentation based on revenue and engagement 2. Identify our "ideal customer profile" based on the characteristics of our highest-value, longest-tenured customers 3. Flag accounts that show warning signs of potential churn (low engagement, declining usage) 4. Which customer segments have the most room for expansion?

HR and Workforce Analysis

> I've uploaded our employee data (anonymized): department, tenure, level, performance rating, compensation band, voluntary turnover flag, engagement survey score.
>
> Analyze for patterns: 1. Where is voluntary turnover highest? Is it correlated with tenure, department, or performance rating? 2. Is there a compensation gap between departments at the same level? 3. What does the tenure distribution look like — are we retaining people past the 2-year mark? 4. Is there a correlation between engagement scores and turnover?

Creating Dashboards and Reports from Data

AI can help you build simple dashboards for ongoing monitoring.

> Based on this data, design a monthly executive dashboard. Tell me: - Which 8-10 metrics should be on the dashboard? - What visualization type is best for each metric? - What thresholds should trigger Red/Yellow/Green status? - What does the layout look like?
>
> Then create the charts for this month's data.

AI-generated charts may not be polished enough for a final dashboard tool (Tableau, Looker, Power BI), but they are excellent for prototyping what the dashboard should look like before you build it in production.

Working with Formulas and Spreadsheets

Even if you are comfortable with spreadsheets, AI can accelerate formula work significantly.

> I have a sales forecast spreadsheet in Excel. I need a formula that: - Takes the average monthly growth rate from the last 6 months - Applies it forward for the next 12 months - Includes a column for a seasonality adjustment factor that I can input manually - Shows the cumulative total for the year
>
> Write the Excel formulas I need and tell me which cells to put them in.

AI-generated Excel formulas tend to be accurate and well-structured. For complex ones, test with a few known values before relying on the calculation.

The Limitations of AI Data Analysis

Where AI data analysis falls short:

Statistical rigor. AI can calculate a correlation coefficient, but it does not always understand whether that correlation is statistically significant or practically meaningful. For high-stakes decisions that require statistical rigor — clinical trials, regulatory compliance, academic research — use proper statistical tools and, ideally, a trained statistician.

Causation vs. correlation. AI is prone to implying causal relationships from correlational data. "Customers who attend onboarding webinars churn less" might be true, but it does not necessarily mean the webinars prevent churn — it might mean engaged customers are both more likely to attend webinars and less likely to churn.

Data quality. AI cannot fix fundamentally bad data. If your CRM is full of duplicate records, incorrect tags, and missing fields, AI will analyze the garbage faithfully and give you garbage insights. Clean data in, good analysis out. Dirty data in, confident-sounding nonsense out.

Complex joins and transformations. If your analysis requires combining data from multiple systems with complex join logic, AI may struggle. Prepare a combined dataset before uploading.

Very large datasets. If your dataset has hundreds of thousands of rows, AI may not process it well due to context window limits. Aggregate first, or use a dedicated analytics tool for the heavy lifting and AI for interpretation.

Making Data-Driven Decisions

The point of data analysis is better decisions. AI helps bridge analysis and action.

> Here is the analysis we've done on our customer churn data. Help me build a recommendation for the leadership team:
>
> 1. Summarize the key findings in 3-4 bullet points
> 2. Translate each finding into a specific, actionable recommendation
> 3. Prioritize the recommendations by expected impact and ease of implementation
> 4. Identify what additional data we would need to validate these recommendations
> 5. Draft the "Key Findings" slide for our executive presentation

The Bottom Line

Data analysis used to be a specialist function. You needed SQL skills, Excel mastery, or a stats degree to pull insight from a spreadsheet. In 2026, you need the ability to ask a good question.

That is a fundamental shift in how business intelligence works. Insight is no longer locked behind technical skills — it is accessible to anyone who can describe what they want to know. Your competitive advantage is no longer in the mechanics of analysis. It is in knowing which questions to ask and what to do with the answers.

AI does not make you a data scientist. It makes data science accessible to people who make business decisions. That is a much bigger deal.

Chapter 9: Market Research

Market research used to be something you either did expensively or did not do at all. You could hire a consulting firm for $50,000 to produce a market landscape report, or hire a research analyst to spend weeks pulling data from industry databases and synthesizing it into something actionable. Or, more commonly, you skipped formal research and relied on intuition, anecdotes from sales calls, and whatever your CEO read in the Wall Street Journal last week.

AI has created a middle path. You can now conduct meaningful market research — competitive analysis, market sizing, trend identification, customer insight synthesis — in hours instead of weeks, at roughly $20 per month instead of $50,000 per engagement. It will not be as rigorous as what a top-tier consulting firm produces, but it will be vastly better than the gut-feeling approach most businesses default to.

This chapter shows you how to use AI for practical market research that informs real decisions.

The AI Research Toolkit

Before diving into specific tasks, a quick orientation on which tools are best for market research.

Perplexity is the standout. It combines AI reasoning with real-time web search and cites its sources, so you can verify what it tells you. For factual research, competitive intelligence, and current market data, Perplexity is your first choice.

ChatGPT and Claude are better for analysis and synthesis. Once you have gathered data, these tools excel at finding patterns, building frameworks, and generating strategic insights. They also handle extended, multi-step research conversations better.

Google Gemini has native integration with Google Search, which makes it useful for research that requires current web information.

Recommended approach: gather with Perplexity (sources), analyze and synthesize with Claude or ChatGPT (thinking), then verify claims independently before deciding anything.

Competitive Analysis

Competitive analysis is the most common market research task in business. AI has made it dramatically more accessible.

The Quick Competitive Scan

When you need a fast overview of your competitive landscape:

> I work for a mid-market HR software company that focuses on performance management and employee engagement. Our main competitors are Lattice, 15Five, Culture Amp, and BambooHR.
>
> For each competitor, give me: 1. Primary product focus and positioning 2. Target customer segment (company size, industry) 3. Pricing model and approximate price points 4. Key differentiators — what do they claim to do better than everyone else? 5. Recent notable moves (funding, acquisitions, product launches, leadership changes) 6. Publicly available growth indicators (customer count, employee count, revenue if public)

Run this through Perplexity for current information. Take the results to Claude or ChatGPT for analysis:

> Based on this competitive overview, analyze: 1. Where is the market heading? What themes are all competitors investing in? 2. Where are the gaps — what are customers asking for that nobody is doing well? 3. How should we position ourselves given this landscape? 4. Which competitor is the biggest threat to us, and why?

The Deep Competitive Dive

For a thorough competitive analysis on a specific competitor:

> I need a deep analysis of [Competitor Name]. Research:
>
> **Product and positioning:** - Full product suite and feature set - How they describe themselves (mission, value proposition) - Recent product

announcements and roadmap hints (from press releases, blog posts, conference talks)

Go-to-market: - Pricing and packaging (tiers, what's included at each level) - Sales model (self-serve, inside sales, enterprise sales) - Marketing channels and messaging themes - Key partnerships and integrations

Market presence: - Estimated number of customers and revenue (use any available data) - Key customer segments and notable logos - Geographic focus - G2/Gartner/Forrester positioning

Strengths and weaknesses: - What do customers consistently praise? (Check G2 reviews, Reddit, social media) - What do customers consistently complain about? - What would you identify as their strategic vulnerabilities?

Monitoring Competitors Over Time

Set up a regular competitive monitoring cadence:

> Every two weeks, I want to do a competitive check-in. Here is my monitoring template. For each competitor, check for:
>
> 1. New product announcements or feature releases
> 2. Pricing changes
> 3. Major customer wins or losses
> 4. Hiring patterns (are they hiring aggressively in any area?)
> 5. Press coverage or analyst mentions
> 6. Social media sentiment shifts
>
> Competitors to monitor: [list]

Market Sizing

Market sizing is one of the most common tasks in business strategy, and one where AI saves enormous time — with an important caveat about precision.

Top-Down Market Sizing

> Help me estimate the total addressable market (TAM) for cloud-based inventory management software targeting mid-market retail companies (50-500 employees) in North America.
>
> Use a top-down approach: 1. How many mid-market retail companies are in North America? 2. What percentage currently use cloud-based inventory management? 3. What is the average annual spend on inventory management software per company? 4. What is the growth rate of this market?
>
> Show your assumptions clearly so I can adjust them. Cite your data sources.

Bottom-Up Market Sizing

> Now approach the same market bottom-up: 1. Start with the number of potential users per company (typically inventory managers, store managers, buyers) 2. Multiply by a reasonable per-seat or per-store pricing model 3. Apply adoption rate estimates based on the maturity of the category 4. Factor in geographic distribution
>
> Compare the bottom-up estimate to our top-down estimate. Where do they agree? Where do they diverge, and what does that tell us?

Important caveat: AI market sizing gives you order of magnitude, not precision. Use it for strategic planning and internal discussions, not investor pitch decks or regulatory filings. Always validate key assumptions with industry reports (IBISWorld, Statista, Gartner) or primary research.

Trend Analysis

Understanding where a market is heading is often more valuable than understanding where it is today.

Industry Trend Identification

> I'm in the commercial real estate industry. Identify the top 10 trends affecting commercial real estate in 2026. For each trend: 1. What is the trend? 2. What is driving it? 3. How mature is it — early, mainstream, or late? 4. What is the business impact? 5. Who is best positioned to

benefit? 6. What should a mid-size commercial brokerage firm do about it?

Technology Trend Assessment

Our company is evaluating whether to invest in building AI capabilities into our product (a project management tool). Help me assess: 1. What AI features are competitors in the PM space launching? 2. What do customers actually want from AI in project management? (Check forums, reviews, surveys) 3. Is AI in PM a genuine value driver or is it table-stakes "we have AI too" marketing? 4. What would a meaningful AI implementation look like vs. a superficial one? 5. What is the risk of not having AI features by 2027?

Emerging Market Identification

We're a B2B SaaS company looking for adjacent markets to enter. Our core competency is workflow automation for financial services.

Identify 5 potential adjacent markets where: - Our existing technology would be applicable - The market is underserved by current solutions - The customer profile is similar enough to our current customers that our sales motion would work - The market is growing at least 15% annually

For each opportunity, estimate the market size and explain the strategic logic.

Customer Research

AI helps you make sense of customer data and feedback at scale.

Voice of Customer Analysis

I have 200 customer feedback responses from our quarterly NPS survey. Analyze them for: 1. Top 5 themes in positive comments (what customers love) 2. Top 5 themes in negative comments (what customers want improved) 3. Differences between promoters (9-10), passives (7-8), and detractors (0-6) 4. Any new themes that weren't present in previous surveys 5. Specific feature requests mentioned by 3 or more respondents 6. Sentiment analysis across customer segments (enterprise vs. mid-market vs. SMB)

Customer Interview Preparation

> I'm conducting customer discovery interviews for a potential new product. We're exploring whether small business owners would pay for an AI-powered bookkeeping assistant.
>
> Help me prepare: 1. An interview guide with 12-15 open-ended questions 2. Questions that uncover pain points without leading the witness 3. Questions that test willingness to pay without directly asking "would you pay for this?" 4. A scoring framework to evaluate responses consistently across interviews

Customer Persona Development

> Based on this data — our CRM records, NPS survey results, and sales call notes — help me develop 3-4 customer personas for our product. For each persona: - Name, title, and company type - Demographics and professional background - Goals and motivations - Key pain points and challenges - How they evaluate and buy software - What messaging resonates with them - Common objections and how to address them

Analyst Report Synthesis

If your company subscribes to industry analyst reports (Gartner, Forrester, IDC), AI helps you extract and synthesize their findings.

> I've uploaded the latest Gartner Magic Quadrant report for our category. Summarize: 1. Where we are positioned and what Gartner says about us 2. Who moved up, down, or entered/exited the quadrant 3. Key buying criteria Gartner identified 4. Trends Gartner highlights for the next 2-3 years 5. Implications for our product strategy and go-to-market approach
>
> Now compare this Gartner report to the Forrester Wave we received last quarter. Where do the analysts agree? Where do they disagree? What should we pay attention to?

Building a Research Brief

When you need to present research to leadership or use it to inform strategy:

I've completed extensive market research over the past two weeks. Here is everything I've gathered: [paste or upload compiled notes, data, and findings]

Help me structure this into a 5-page market research brief with:

1. Executive summary (half page)
2. Market overview — size, growth, key players
3. Competitive landscape — positioning map, key insights
4. Customer insights — what buyers want, how they buy
5. Trends and implications — what's changing and what it means for us
6. Strategic recommendations — 3-5 specific actions we should take

Include charts or tables where they would strengthen the narrative.

Research Integrity

AI-assisted research is powerful but carries risks you have to manage.

Verify factual claims. AI sometimes cites statistics that are outdated, inaccurate, or completely fabricated. For any number that matters to your decision, find the original source and confirm it. Perplexity's citations help, but even cited sources should be spot-checked.

Be aware of training data limitations. AI's knowledge has a cutoff date and may not reflect the very latest developments. For current market data, supplement AI analysis with real-time sources: press releases, SEC filings, LinkedIn job postings (as a proxy for company growth), and industry news.

Distinguish analysis from opinion. When AI tells you "the market is shifting toward consolidation," that might be a well-supported observation or a pattern-matched guess. Ask for evidence. "What specific data points support that conclusion?"

Primary research still matters. AI synthesizes secondary research rapidly, but it cannot replace the insights you get from talking to actual customers, prospects, and industry experts. Use AI research as the foundation, then validate and enrich with primary conversations.

The Small Business Advantage

Worth highlighting: AI-powered market research is perhaps most transformative for small businesses and startups.

Large companies have always had access to market research — analyst subscriptions, research teams, consulting budgets. Small businesses had to compete without that intelligence.

AI levels the playing field significantly. A two-person startup can now produce market research that is 80 percent as good as what a large company's strategy team produces, at roughly 0.1 percent of the cost. That does not erase the advantage of a dedicated research team, but it dramatically narrows the gap.

If you are a small business owner or entrepreneur, this chapter's techniques are some of the highest-leverage AI applications available to you.

The Bottom Line

Market research is the foundation of good strategy. You cannot make smart decisions about products, positioning, pricing, or expansion without understanding your market, your competitors, and your customers.

AI has not changed that. What it has changed is who can do market research and how fast. A task that used to require specialized skills and significant budget now requires a well-crafted prompt and a few hours of focused work.

The research will not be perfect. It will contain gaps, biases, and occasional inaccuracies. But it will be vastly better than no research at all, which is what most businesses were doing before.

Use AI to make market intelligence a regular practice, not an occasional luxury. The businesses that understand their markets best are the ones that win.

Part IV: Business Functions

"Business has only two functions — marketing and innovation."

— Milan Kundera (attributed to Peter Drucker)

Chapter 10: Marketing and Content

Marketing is where AI has made perhaps its most visible impact on business. Walk into any marketing department in 2026 and you will find AI woven into the daily workflow — drafting social posts, analyzing campaign performance, generating ad copy variations, building content calendars, helping teams produce more content across more channels than was humanly possible two years ago.

This is both the opportunity and the risk. The opportunity is obvious: AI lets marketing teams punch above their weight, producing more content of higher quality with less effort. The risk is less obvious but equally important: when every company has the same tools, using AI to produce content is not a competitive advantage. The advantage comes from using it strategically — to produce better content, not just more of it.

This chapter covers both: how to use AI to accelerate your marketing work, and how to make sure the result is actually good.

Content Strategy

Before you write a word, AI helps you figure out what to write and why.

Content Calendar Planning

> I'm the content marketing manager for a B2B cybersecurity company. Our target audience is IT directors and CISOs at mid-market companies (500-5,000 employees). We publish 3 blog posts per week, 1 whitepaper per month, and post daily on LinkedIn.
>
> Help me plan a content calendar for Q2 2026. Consider: - Key industry events and conferences in Q2 - Seasonal themes (budget planning season, compliance deadlines) - Our product launch of a new endpoint detection feature in May - Top SEO keywords in our space - Content gaps based on what our competitors are publishing
>
> Create a week-by-week calendar with topics, formats, target keywords, and target personas.

Content Audit

> Here are the titles and performance metrics (page views, time on page, conversion rate) for our last 50 blog posts. Analyze: 1. Which topics consistently perform best? 2. What content formats (how-to, listicle, thought leadership, case study) drive the most engagement? 3. What is our optimal post length based on performance data? 4. Are there topics we've covered too much or not enough? 5. What patterns do you see in our top 10 vs. bottom 10 posts?

Competitive Content Analysis

> Analyze the content marketing approach of our top 3 competitors. For each one: - What topics do they cover most frequently? - What formats do they use (blogs, whitepapers, videos, podcasts)? - How often do they publish? - What is their tone and style? - Where do they seem to get the most engagement? - What are they NOT covering that we could own?

Blog and Article Writing

AI-assisted blog writing is the most mature marketing application of AI. Here is how to do it well.

The Right Way to Use AI for Blog Posts

Be direct about this: having AI write an entire blog post from a one-line prompt produces generic, forgettable content. It reads like AI wrote it because AI did write it, with no human insight added.

The right approach uses AI as an accelerator for your expertise, not a replacement.

Step 1: Bring Your Insight

Start with something you know that your audience does not. A trend you have observed, a mistake you keep seeing customers make, a counterintuitive lesson from your experience. The human insight is what makes content worth reading.

> I want to write a blog post about why most companies' cybersecurity training programs fail. My core argument is that the problem isn't the training content — it's the delivery model. One-and-done annual

> training doesn't change behavior. What works is continuous micro-training integrated into daily workflow.
>
> I have specific examples from three clients who switched to this model and saw phishing click rates drop by 60-70%.

Step 2: Let AI Structure and Draft

> Based on that thesis, outline a 1,200-word blog post that: - Opens with a provocative statistic or scenario - Presents the conventional approach and why it fails - Introduces the alternative approach with evidence - Includes practical steps the reader can take - Ends with a clear takeaway
>
> Target audience: IT directors who are frustrated with their current security awareness program.

Step 3: Review, Inject Your Voice, and Polish

Read the draft critically. Add your examples. Adjust tone to match your brand. Remove AI-isms (you will learn to spot them — phrases like "in today's rapidly evolving threat landscape" are dead giveaways). Add your own turns of phrase and personality.

The result: a blog post that combines AI's structural competence with your domain expertise and authentic voice. Thirty minutes instead of three hours.

SEO-Optimized Content

> I'm writing a blog post targeting the keyword "employee onboarding checklist." Help me: 1. Identify related keywords and LSI terms I should include 2. Analyze the top 5 ranking articles for this keyword — what do they cover? 3. What angle can we take that's different from what's already ranking? 4. Write a meta title and meta description optimized for click-through rate 5. Suggest an H2 structure that covers the topic comprehensively while naturally incorporating target keywords

Social Media Content

Social media is where AI's volume really shines — and where the temptation to over-automate is strongest.

LinkedIn Posts

LinkedIn has become the dominant B2B social platform, and it rewards specific, experience-based content. How to use AI effectively for it:

> Write a LinkedIn post based on this idea: I just had a client meeting where they asked me to justify the cost of our data analytics platform. Instead of pulling out our ROI calculator, I asked them one question: "What was the last strategic decision your team made based on a spreadsheet analysis?" They couldn't name one. The tool isn't expensive — the cost of not using data for decisions is expensive.
>
> Write this as a conversational LinkedIn post. Short paragraphs (1-2 sentences each). Start with a hook. Include a clear insight. End with a question to drive engagement. Maximum 150 words.

Social Media Batch Creation

> I need to promote our upcoming webinar "5 Signs Your Cybersecurity Stack Is Outdated" across LinkedIn, X/Twitter, and our email newsletter.
>
> Create: - 5 LinkedIn post variations (different angles, different hooks) - 5 tweets/X posts (different angles, under 280 characters each) - 3 email subject lines with preview text - A 100-word email body for newsletter promotion
>
> The webinar is on April 15 at 2 PM ET. Registration link: [link]. Speaker is our CISO, Maria Santos.

Content Repurposing

One of the highest-leverage AI marketing applications: taking one piece of content and spinning it into multiple formats.

> I just published a 2,000-word blog post on supply chain risk management. Repurpose it into: 1. A LinkedIn article (800 words, more opinionated tone) 2. 5 LinkedIn text posts (each highlighting a different insight from the article) 3. An email newsletter summary (200 words with a link to the full post) 4. A Twitter/X thread (8-10 tweets) 5. A slide outline for a 5-minute video or webinar segment 6. 3 potential infographic concepts based on the data in the article

One blog post becomes fifteen pieces of content across five channels. A multiplication factor that would be impossible without AI.

Ad Copy

AI is remarkably effective at generating ad copy variations, which makes A/B testing far more practical.

Google Ads

> Write 10 Google Search ad variations for our project management software targeting small businesses. Each ad needs: - Headline 1 (30 characters max) - Headline 2 (30 characters max) - Headline 3 (30 characters max) - Description 1 (90 characters max) - Description 2 (90 characters max)
>
> Target keyword: "project management software small business" Key selling points: easy to use, free trial, under $10/user/month, no credit card required
>
> Vary the emotional appeals: efficiency, simplicity, affordability, team alignment, stress reduction.

Facebook/Instagram Ads

> Create 5 Facebook ad copy variations for our online course "Financial Planning for Freelancers." Each variation should: - Use a different hook (pain point, aspiration, social proof, curiosity, urgency) - Include primary text (125 words max) - Include a headline (40 characters max) - Include a link description (30 characters max)
>
> Target audience: freelancers and independent contractors aged 25-45 who earn $50K-$150K annually and are anxious about financial stability.

Email Marketing

Campaign Emails

> Write a 3-email nurture sequence for leads who downloaded our whitepaper on "AI in Manufacturing."

Email 1 (send day 0): Thank them, summarize key takeaways, position our company as a thought leader Email 2 (send day 3): Share a related case study, include a specific result (company X reduced defect rates by 34%) Email 3 (send day 7): Soft offer — invite to a consultation or demo, make it low pressure

Tone: knowledgeable, helpful, not pushy. Subject lines should prioritize open rates.

Subject Line Generation

Generate 20 subject line options for our monthly product update newsletter. This month's key updates are: - New reporting dashboard - Slack integration (most requested feature) - Updated pricing (10% decrease for annual plans)

Give me a mix of styles: straightforward, curiosity-driven, emoji (tasteful), question-based, and number-based. Max 50 characters each.

Brand Voice and Consistency

One of marketing's hardest tasks is maintaining a consistent brand voice across multiple writers, channels, and content types. AI helps.

Brand Voice Documentation

I'm going to give you 10 examples of marketing content we've written that represents our brand voice at its best. Analyze these and create a brand voice guide that includes:

1. Voice attributes (3-5 adjectives that describe our tone)
2. Language dos and don'ts (specific words and phrases we use and avoid)
3. Sentence structure patterns
4. Humor guidelines (how much, what kind)
5. Examples of on-brand vs. off-brand versions of the same message

This guide will be used by AI tools and human writers to maintain consistency.

Voice Consistency Check

Review this draft blog post against our brand voice guide [paste guide]. Flag any sections that drift from our brand voice and suggest revisions.

Marketing Analytics

AI helps marketing teams get more insight from their data.

> Here is our marketing performance data for Q1. Analyze and answer: 1. Which channels have the best CAC (customer acquisition cost)? 2. How does our content marketing funnel look — where are we losing people? 3. Are there diminishing returns on any channel (spending more but not getting proportionally more results)? 4. What does our data suggest we should invest more in next quarter? What should we pull back from? 5. How does our performance compare to typical B2B SaaS benchmarks?

The Authenticity Challenge

The elephant in the room: customers can increasingly tell when content is AI-generated, and many do not like it.

The symptoms are becoming familiar: perfect grammar with no personality, generic insights that could apply to any company, buzzword-heavy openings, and a relentless positivity that feels disconnected from reality.

The antidote is not to stop using AI. It is to use AI as an accelerator for genuine human expertise, not a replacement. The best AI-assisted marketing content has three qualities:

1. **A specific, opinionated point of view.** AI can help you express your ideas; it should not be the source of them.
2. **Real examples from real experience.** AI generates hypothetical examples. You have actual ones. Use them.
3. **Honest imperfection.** Perfect, polished, hedge-free content often reads as AI-generated precisely because humans are not perfect, polished, and hedge-free. A little personality, a little self-deprecation, a willingness to say "I'm not sure but here's what I think" — these are markers of authentic human writing.

The Bottom Line

AI has given marketing teams superpowers. More content, more variations tested, more data analyzed, consistency across more channels — these are genuine capabilities that translate to real business results.

But the strategic layer — knowing what to say, who to say it to, and why it matters — is still human territory. AI is the execution engine. You are the strategist.

The marketing teams that win in 2026 are not the ones that produce the most content. They are the ones that produce the most relevant, authentic, strategically sound content — and use AI to do it at a pace their competitors cannot match.

Chapter 11: Sales and Customer Relations

Sales is a human endeavor. People buy from people they trust, and no amount of AI can replicate the relationship-building, emotional intelligence, and situational awareness that close deals. But here is the paradox: the average salesperson spends only 28 percent of their time actually selling. The rest goes to CRM updates, email follow-ups, proposal writing, research, internal meetings, and administrative tasks that are necessary but do not directly generate revenue.

AI attacks that 72 percent. It handles the research, the writing, the admin, and the prep — freeing salespeople to do what only humans can do: build relationships and close deals.

Prospecting and Lead Research

The first step in any sales process is understanding who you are selling to. AI compresses hours of research into minutes.

Company Research

> I have a discovery call tomorrow with Sarah Chen, VP of Operations at Pacific Ridge Logistics. They're a mid-size freight logistics company based in Portland, OR, approximately 350 employees, primarily serving e-commerce and retail clients.
>
> Help me prepare: 1. Company overview — what does Pacific Ridge do, who are their key clients, what is their market position? 2. Industry context — what are the top challenges in freight logistics right now? 3. Likely pain points for a VP of Operations at this type of company 4. Our product's relevance — we sell workforce management software. What specific problems of theirs could we address? 5. Intelligent questions to ask that show I've done my homework 6. Potential objections and how to handle them

For the most current information, run the company research through Perplexity. For the strategic preparation — pain points, objections, questions — use Claude or ChatGPT.

Contact Research

> Research Sarah Chen (VP Operations, Pacific Ridge Logistics). Check LinkedIn, company website, industry publications. I need: - Her professional background and career path - Any published articles, conference talks, or interviews - Topics she's commented on or shared on LinkedIn - Mutual connections or shared interests - Anything that would help me build rapport in the first two minutes of our call

Lead List Enrichment

> I have a list of 50 target companies. For each one, I need: - Industry and sub-industry - Employee count (approximate) - Key decision-makers (titles of people who typically buy workforce management software) - Likely technology stack - Any recent news or trigger events (funding, expansion, leadership changes, acquisitions)
>
> Here is the list: [paste company names]

Outreach

Cold outreach is one of the hardest tasks in sales. AI helps you craft messages that feel personal without burning thirty minutes on each one.

Personalized Cold Emails

> Write a cold outreach email to Sarah Chen. I want to reference: - Pacific Ridge's recent expansion into last-mile delivery (I saw this in their press release) - The workforce management challenges that come with adding delivery drivers (scheduling, compliance, time tracking) - Our solution's specific feature for logistics companies (automated DOT compliance scheduling)
>
> Keep it under 120 words. No salesy language. Open with something relevant to her specifically, not "I hope this email finds you well." Make the ask a simple question, not a meeting request.

The key to AI-assisted cold email is specificity. "I'd love to show you how we can help your business" is generic AI output. "I noticed Pacific Ridge is expanding into last-mile delivery — that usually means a DOT compliance scheduling headache for new drivers" is specific, relevant, and earns a response.

Follow-Up Sequences

> Create a 4-touch follow-up sequence for prospects who don't respond to my initial email. Each touch should: - Use a different angle (value, social proof, curiosity, direct ask) - Be shorter than the previous one - Not be annoying or guilt-trippy - Reference the original email without re-sending it - Spaced at days 3, 7, 14, and 21 after the initial email
>
> Context: I'm selling to VP/Director-level operations leaders at logistics companies.

LinkedIn Outreach

> Write a LinkedIn connection request message (max 300 characters) to David Okonkwo, Director of IT at Cascade Distribution. I want to mention our shared interest in supply chain technology (he posted about it last week) and offer to share our recent industry benchmark report.

Proposals and Presentations

Sales proposals are where AI delivers the most dramatic time savings in the sales workflow.

Custom Proposals

> I need to create a proposal for Pacific Ridge Logistics based on our discovery call. Here's what I learned:
>
> **Their situation:** - 350 employees across 4 locations, expanding to 6 by year-end - Currently using spreadsheets and a legacy system for scheduling - Spending ~20 hours/week on manual scheduling across locations - DOT compliance tracking is manual and they've had two near-misses in audits - High driver turnover (38% annually), partly due to scheduling frustration

Their priorities: - Automated scheduling that accounts for DOT requirements - Mobile access for drivers - Visibility across all locations - Cost control (they're budget-conscious)

Our solution: - WorkForce Pro platform at $12/user/month - DOT compliance module (included) - Implementation: 6-8 weeks - Expected to save 15+ hours/week on scheduling - Similar customer case study: TransWest Freight reduced scheduling time by 70% and driver turnover by 22%

Write a professional proposal that leads with their pain, positions our solution against it, includes the case study as proof, and closes with a clear pricing and next-steps section. Maximum 6 pages.

Proposal Review and Strengthening

Review this proposal and help me strengthen it: 1. Is the value proposition clear in the first page? 2. Are we leading with features or with outcomes? (We should lead with outcomes.) 3. Is the pricing section positioned well? Should I move it? 4. What objections might this proposal raise, and how can I preempt them? 5. Is the ask clear — does the reader know exactly what to do next?

RFP Responses

I've uploaded this 40-page RFP from a potential client. Help me: 1. Extract every requirement and organize them into a response matrix 2. Identify requirements we meet fully, partially, or don't meet 3. Draft responses for requirements we fully meet, using our product documentation as source material 4. Flag requirements we don't meet and suggest how to address them in our response 5. Write the executive summary section of our response

CRM and Pipeline Management

AI helps keep your CRM clean and your pipeline accurate.

Call Notes to CRM Updates

After every sales call, instead of spending ten minutes on CRM updates:

Here are my rough notes from my call with Sarah Chen at Pacific Ridge. Convert these into a structured CRM update: - Meeting summary (2-3 sentences) - Key findings and pain points discussed - Next steps with dates - Deal stage recommendation - Likelihood to close (based on buying signals in the notes) - Follow-up tasks to create

Format this so I can paste it directly into Salesforce.

Pipeline Analysis

Here is our current pipeline data. Analyze and give me: 1. Which deals are most likely to close this month and why? 2. Which deals are stalled (no activity in 14+ days)? 3. What is our realistic forecast vs. our optimistic forecast? 4. Are we top-heavy (too many early-stage deals) or bottom-heavy? 5. Based on our average conversion rates, do we have enough pipeline to hit our Q2 target?

Win/Loss Analysis

Here are the details on our last 20 closed deals (10 wins, 10 losses). For each, I've noted the deal size, industry, competitor, decision factors, and outcome.

Analyze for patterns: 1. What do our wins have in common? 2. What do our losses have in common? 3. Where are we losing to specific competitors, and why? 4. Is deal size correlated with win rate? 5. What should our ideal customer profile be based on this data?

Customer Communication

Meeting Prep

I have a quarterly business review with our largest customer, Westfield Manufacturing ($180K ARR). Prepare: 1. An agenda for a 60-minute QBR 2. Talking points for their usage metrics (I'll provide the data) 3. Expansion opportunity brief (they're adding a new plant — how does this affect their needs?) 4. Risk assessment — are there any signs they might churn? 5. Three questions to ask that uncover expansion opportunities

Renewal and Upsell Communications

Draft a renewal conversation guide for the following account. Contract expires in 60 days. They've been a good customer for 2 years but have had some support issues in Q4.

I need: 1. A value recap email — reminding them of the ROI they've achieved 2. Talking points for the renewal call that address the Q4 support issues proactively 3. An upsell pitch for our analytics module (natural next step given their maturity) 4. A pricing discussion framework (they'll likely ask for a discount)

Handling Difficult Customer Situations

We delivered a project late and over budget for a key account. The client's VP of IT is frustrated and has requested a meeting. Help me: 1. Write a pre-meeting email acknowledging the issues 2. Prepare talking points for the meeting that take responsibility without groveling 3. Draft a remediation plan with specific actions and timelines 4. Create a "make-good" offer that demonstrates our commitment (without giving away too much margin) 5. Write the follow-up email documenting our commitments

Sales Enablement

Battle Cards

Create a competitive battle card for when we're up against [Competitor]. Include: - Their strengths (be honest) - Their weaknesses (be specific) - Feature-by-feature comparison on the 10 features that matter most - Killer questions to ask the prospect that expose the competitor's weaknesses - Objection handling: when the prospect says "but [competitor] has X," here's how to respond - Proof points: customer stories where we won against this competitor

Objection Handling Guide

Our sales team keeps encountering the same 10 objections. For each one, create a response framework:

1. "Your product is too expensive"
2. "We're happy with our current solution"

3. “We don’t have budget until next fiscal year”
4. “I need to get buy-in from my team”
5. “Can you match [competitor’s] price?”
6. “We tried something similar and it didn’t work”
7. “We don’t have the resources to implement”
8. “What happens if we outgrow your platform?”
9. “We need [feature you don’t have]”
10. “Just send me some information and I’ll review it”

   For each objection, provide: what the prospect is really saying, how to respond, a follow-up question to keep the conversation moving, and a real-world example of overcoming this objection.

AI-Powered CRM Features

Most major CRM platforms now include AI features worth knowing about.

Salesforce Einstein provides lead scoring, opportunity insights, email sentiment analysis, and automated data entry. It is deeply integrated into the Salesforce workflow and works best for organizations already invested in that ecosystem.

HubSpot AI offers content generation, predictive lead scoring, conversation intelligence (analyzing sales calls for coaching opportunities), and automated meeting scheduling. It is especially accessible for small and mid-market sales teams.

Microsoft Dynamics Copilot embeds AI directly into the Dynamics 365 CRM workflow, offering email drafting, meeting preparation, and opportunity summarization.

These built-in features complement the general-purpose AI tools we have been discussing. The CRM AI handles data-rich tasks inside the CRM workflow; the general-purpose tools handle the thinking, writing, and strategy work that happens outside it.

The Human Element

The most important point about AI in sales is this: it makes sales more human, not less.

The irony is that AI's greatest contribution is freeing salespeople to be more human. When you are not spending hours on research, email drafting, CRM updates, and proposal writing, you have more time for the work that actually builds relationships and closes deals: listening to customers, understanding their real problems, thinking creatively about solutions, and following through on commitments.

The salesperson who uses AI to spend 50 percent of their time selling instead of 28 percent is not being replaced by technology. They are being unleashed by it.

That is the sales professional of 2026: AI-assisted in preparation, deeply human in execution.

Chapter 12: Human Resources

> **Important:** AI is not an HR professional or employment lawyer, and nothing in this chapter constitutes legal or HR compliance advice. Employment practices vary by jurisdiction. Always verify AI-generated HR content with qualified professionals.

HR has a unique challenge with AI: HR professionals are both users of AI tools and stewards of AI policy for their organizations. This chapter focuses on the first role — how you, as an HR professional, can use AI to be more effective. Chapter 20 covers organizational adoption, and Chapter 22 addresses the ethical considerations HR teams need to champion.

The scope of HR work is enormous, and much of it is writing. Job descriptions, offer letters, policies, handbooks, onboarding materials, performance review frameworks, training content, internal communications, investigation summaries, compliance documentation. AI accelerates all of it.

Recruiting and Talent Acquisition

Recruiting is one of HR's most time-intensive functions, and AI helps at every stage.

Job Descriptions

Job descriptions may be the single most common document AI writes better than most humans. The reason is simple: most job descriptions are terrible. They are padded with vague requirements, stuffed with jargon, and fail to communicate what the job actually involves or why anyone would want it.

> Write a job description for a Senior Product Manager at a B2B SaaS company (200 employees, project management software). This role reports to the VP of Product and manages 2 associate PMs.
>
> Requirements: - 5+ years of product management experience in B2B SaaS - Experience with agile methodologies - Strong analytical skills (SQL is a plus but not required) - Excellent communication skills (this person presents to the exec team monthly)

Include: - What this person will actually do day-to-day (be specific, not vague) - What success looks like in the first 90 days, 6 months, and year - Team context — who they work with - Compensation range: $135K-$165K base + equity + benefits - What makes this role different from a PM role at a bigger company (more ownership, closer to customers, faster pace)

Style: conversational, direct, no corporate jargon. We want to attract builders, not bureaucrats.

Compare this to the typical approach: copy last year's job description and change a few words. The AI-generated version will be more specific, more compelling, and more likely to attract the right candidates.

Inclusive Job Descriptions

Review this job description for language that might discourage diverse candidates from applying. Check for: - Gendered language - Unnecessarily aggressive terms ("crush it," "rock star," "ninja") - Requirements that are actually preferences in disguise - Qualifications that create unnecessary barriers (does this really require a degree?) - Language that assumes a specific cultural background

Suggest specific revisions for each issue found.

Interview Question Development

Design a structured interview for the Senior Product Manager role. Create:

1. Phone screen questions (15 minutes, focus on fit and basic qualifications)
2. Technical interview questions (45 minutes, assess product thinking, analytical skills, prioritization)
3. Behavioral interview questions (45 minutes, assess leadership, communication, collaboration)
4. Culture fit questions (30 minutes, assess alignment with our values of ownership, transparency, and customer obsession)

For each question, provide: - The question itself - What a strong answer looks like - What a weak answer looks like - A follow-up probe question - The competency being assessed

Interview Scheduling and Coordination

I need to coordinate a full interview loop for 3 candidates for the Senior PM role. Each candidate needs: - 30-min phone screen with recruiter - 45-min product exercise with hiring manager - 45-min behavioral interview with VP Product - 30-min team fit chat with 2 associate PMs - 30-min executive conversation with CTO

Draft the scheduling emails: 1. To the candidate — inviting them to the interview loop, explaining each stage 2. To each internal interviewer — with the candidate's resume summary, role context, and their specific interview focus 3. A debrief meeting invite for all interviewers after the loop completes

Candidate Evaluation

Here are the interview scorecards from 5 interviewers for candidate Maria Lopez. Summarize: 1. Areas of unanimous agreement (positive and negative) 2. Areas where interviewers disagreed — what did some see that others didn't? 3. Key strengths and concerns 4. An overall recommendation based on the collective feedback 5. Specific questions to address in the debrief discussion

Offer Letters

Draft an offer letter for Maria Lopez for the Senior Product Manager position. Include: - Position title and start date (April 21, 2026) - Compensation: $155K base, 15% target bonus, 5,000 stock options (4-year vest, 1-year cliff) - Benefits summary (standard package: medical/dental/vision, 401k with 4% match, unlimited PTO) - Reporting structure - At-will employment language - Expiration date for the offer (5 business days)

Tone: welcoming and enthusiastic. We want her to feel excited about joining.

Onboarding

AI helps create comprehensive onboarding programs that actually set new hires up for success.

Onboarding Plan Creation

Design a 90-day onboarding plan for a Senior Product Manager joining our team. Structure it as:

Week 1: Orientation - People to meet (with context on each person's role and why the meeting matters) - Systems and tools to set up - Documents to read - Cultural norms to absorb

Weeks 2-4: Learning - Product deep dives - Customer calls to shadow - Team processes to understand - First small deliverable

Months 2-3: Contributing - Increasing ownership of specific areas - First independent project - 30-day and 60-day check-in agendas - 90-day assessment criteria

Welcome Materials

Create a "New Hire Welcome Guide" for our company. Include: - Company history and mission (brief, not boring) - Organizational structure and key people - How we communicate (Slack etiquette, email expectations, meeting culture) - Benefits and perks explained simply (not legalese) - Common first-week questions and answers - A glossary of internal acronyms and terminology

Tone: friendly, practical, the kind of thing you'd want on your first day.

Performance Management

Performance Review Framework

Design a performance review framework for our 200-person company. We want to move away from annual reviews to a more continuous feedback model. Requirements:

- Quarterly lightweight check-ins (30 minutes, structured but not bureaucratic)
- Annual comprehensive review (more thorough, tied to compensation)
- Self-assessment component
- Manager assessment component
- Peer feedback (optional but encouraged)
- Clear rating scale with definitions that minimize subjectivity

> Create templates for each component.

Writing Performance Reviews

This is one of the tasks managers dread most, and AI helps significantly. The key is feeding it specific observations, not asking it to generate a review from nothing.

> I need to write a performance review for one of my direct reports. Here are my notes on their performance this year:
>
> Strengths: consistently delivers on time, great relationship with the engineering team, took ownership of the analytics dashboard project and delivered it under budget, mentored a junior team member effectively.
>
> Areas for growth: tends to avoid conflict — when there's disagreement with stakeholders, she accommodates rather than advocating for her position. Her presentations to the executive team could be more concise and structured. She should be taking on more strategic projects rather than executing on tasks others define.
>
> Write a balanced performance review that: - Is specific and example-based, not generic - Frames growth areas constructively - Includes clear development goals with measurable outcomes - Is honest without being demoralizing

Performance Improvement Plans

When performance management escalates, AI helps create clear, fair documentation.

> Draft a Performance Improvement Plan (PIP) for an employee who is not meeting expectations in these areas: 1. Missed 4 of the last 6 project deadlines 2. Quality of written deliverables has declined — last two client reports required significant revision 3. Has not completed two required compliance training modules
>
> The PIP should include: - Specific behaviors and outcomes that need to change - Measurable goals for each area - Timeline (60 days) - Support and resources provided (weekly 1:1s, writing coaching, protected time for training) - Consequences if goals are not met - Documentation of previous conversations about these issues

Tone: factual, clear, fair. This is not punitive — it's a genuine effort to help them succeed.

Policy Development

Employee Handbook

Review our employee handbook (uploaded) and identify: 1. Policies that are outdated (reference old technologies, practices, or legal frameworks) 2. Sections that are unclear or could be misinterpreted 3. Common handbook sections we're missing 4. Language that's overly legalistic and could be simplified 5. Inconsistencies between different sections

AI Usage Policy

This is the HR policy every organization needs in 2026.

Draft an AI Usage Policy for our company (200 employees, B2B SaaS). The policy should cover:

1. Approved AI tools (we provide licenses for ChatGPT Team and Copilot)
2. Data classification — what can and cannot be shared with AI tools
3. Client data handling — explicit prohibition on sharing client PII with AI
4. Content review requirements — AI-generated content for clients must be reviewed by a human
5. Intellectual property — who owns AI-assisted work product?
6. Transparency — when should we disclose AI use?
7. Bias awareness — be alert to AI biases, especially in HR applications
8. Not a surveillance tool — we're not monitoring individual AI usage

Strike a balance between enabling productivity and managing risk. We want to encourage AI use, not discourage it.

Remote Work Policy

Draft a remote/hybrid work policy for our company. We're moving to a hybrid model: 2 days in-office (Tuesday and Thursday), 3 days remote. This applies to all non-warehouse employees.

Cover: - Core hours (10 AM - 3 PM in employee's time zone) - Home office requirements and stipend ($500/year for equipment) -

Communication expectations - Meeting etiquette for hybrid meetings - Exceptions process - Equipment and IT support

Tone: trust-based, not surveillance-based. We want to attract great people, not micromanage them.

Employee Communications

Sensitive Announcements

Help me draft a company-wide announcement about a reorganization. Key points: - We're combining the Sales and Marketing teams under a single Chief Revenue Officer - The current VP of Marketing, James, is leaving the company (his choice, amicable) - The current VP of Sales, Karen, is being promoted to CRO - No other roles are being eliminated - We're doing this to align our go-to-market effort, not because something is broken

This needs to acknowledge the emotional reality that change is unsettling while projecting confidence in the direction. Mention James's contributions. Be honest that there will be adjustments. Invite questions.

Benefits Communications

Our benefits open enrollment is coming up. We're making two changes this year: 1. Adding a mental health benefit — 6 free therapy sessions per year through a partner 2. Increasing employee 401k match from 3% to 4%

Write: - An announcement email that leads with what employees care about (what's new, what's better) - A FAQ document covering the most likely questions - A one-page comparison showing this year's benefits vs. last year's

HR Data and Analytics

Workforce Analytics

Here is our workforce data for the past 12 months. Analyze: 1. Turnover rate by department — where is it highest? 2. Average tenure by department and level 3. Diversity metrics across the organization and by level 4. Promotion rates — are they equitable across demographics? 5. Correlation between engagement survey scores and turnover 6. Compensation benchmarking — are we competitive in key roles?

Compensation Analysis

Analyze our compensation data for pay equity. Look at: 1. Compensation differences by gender and ethnicity at the same level and role 2. Are there outliers that need investigation? 3. How do our ranges compare to market data? 4. Create a summary suitable for presenting to leadership

Important Cautions for HR AI Use

AI in HR requires particular care because the stakes involve people's livelihoods, careers, and well-being.

Never use AI to make final hiring or firing decisions. AI can help organize information and draft documents, but the decision itself must be made by humans who can account for the full context.

Be aware of bias. AI models can perpetuate biases in their training data. This is especially concerning in recruiting (screening resumes, scoring candidates) and performance management. Always review AI-assisted HR decisions for potential bias.

Protect employee data. Employee data is among the most sensitive information in your organization. Use only enterprise-tier AI tools with appropriate data protection guarantees. Never upload employee personal information to free AI tools.

Maintain the human touch. Some HR conversations — delivering difficult news, counseling an employee through a challenge, celebrating an achievement — should never be delegated to AI. AI helps you prepare for these conversations. It should not conduct them.

The Bottom Line

HR touches every person in the organization, and the quality of HR work directly affects employee experience, retention, and productivity. AI helps HR professionals produce better work — clearer job descriptions, more structured interviews, more comprehensive onboarding, more consistent performance management, more thoughtful policies — while cutting the writing and administrative burden that makes the job exhausting.

The HR professional of 2026 uses AI to handle the production work so they can focus on the people work. That is not a diminishment of the role. It is an elevation of it.

Chapter 13: Finance and Accounting

> **Important:** AI is not an accountant or financial advisor, and nothing in this chapter constitutes financial, tax, or accounting advice. Always verify AI output with qualified professionals.

Finance professionals tend to approach AI with a healthy combination of interest and caution. Interest because finance involves enormous volumes of data, repetitive analysis, and report generation — all areas where AI excels. Caution because finance demands accuracy, and a hallucinated number in a financial report is not just embarrassing — it can be legally consequential.

That caution is well-placed, and I want to honor it in this chapter. AI is genuinely useful for finance and accounting work, but it demands more discipline than some other business functions. The rule is simple: use AI to accelerate your work, never to replace your verification.

Where AI Fits in Finance

A spectrum of finance tasks, and where AI helps most:

High AI value, lower risk: Report narrative writing, expense categorization, data visualization, meeting prep, communication drafting, policy documentation, training materials.

High AI value, moderate risk: Budget analysis, variance explanations, trend identification, financial modeling structure (not the numbers themselves), benchmarking research.

Use with extreme caution: Tax calculations, regulatory compliance determinations, audit documentation, anything that will be filed with a regulatory body. AI can draft these, but every detail must be verified by a qualified professional.

Do not rely on AI for: Legal interpretations of tax code, binding compliance opinions, or any output that substitutes for professional financial advice. AI is a tool, not a CPA.

Financial Reporting

Narrative Report Writing

This is the highest-ROI use of AI in finance. Numbers tell a story, but most financial reports need a human-readable narrative alongside the tables and charts. AI writes these narratives quickly and well.

> Here is our Q1 financial data: - Revenue: $4.2M (vs. $3.8M Q1 last year, +10.5%) - Gross margin: 68% (vs. 71% last year) - Operating expenses: $2.4M (vs. $2.1M last year, +14.3%) - EBITDA: $460K (vs. $580K last year, -20.7%) - Cash: $3.1M (vs. $2.8M at end of Q4) - Headcount: 95 (vs. 82 at end of Q1 last year)
>
> Write the narrative section of our quarterly financial report. Explain: 1. Revenue growth drivers (new enterprise deals drove most of the growth) 2. Why gross margin declined (increased hosting costs from scaling our infrastructure) 3. OpEx increase (13 new hires, primarily in engineering and sales) 4. EBITDA decline in context (planned investment phase, expected to improve as new revenue ramps) 5. Cash position and runway
>
> Audience: board of directors. Tone: confident but honest. They will see the numbers — the narrative should explain them, not spin them.

Variance Analysis

> Here is our budget vs. actual for Q1. For each line item with a variance greater than 5%, write a brief explanation of the variance and whether it's a one-time item or likely to recur.
>
> Format as a table with columns: Line Item | Budget | Actual | Variance ($) | Variance (%) | Explanation | Recurring?

Board Financial Package

> Help me prepare the financial section of our board package. I need:
>
> 1. An executive financial summary (1 page) — key metrics, trends, and the headline story
> 2. Detailed P&L with YoY comparison and commentary
> 3. Cash flow summary and 12-month projection narrative

4. Revenue analysis by segment (enterprise, mid-market, SMB) with commentary
5. Key metrics dashboard content (ARR, MRR, churn rate, CAC, LTV, burn rate)

Here is the raw data: [upload spreadsheet]

Budgeting and Forecasting

Budget Building

I'm building the 2027 annual budget. Help me create a budget template that includes:

- Revenue projections by product line (I'll provide assumptions)
- COGS by category
- Department-level operating expenses
- Headcount plan with loaded costs
- Capital expenditures
- Monthly cash flow projection

Also create a list of assumptions I need to document (growth rates, hiring timeline, pricing changes, etc.) and a sensitivity analysis framework showing how the bottom line changes if key assumptions vary by +/- 10-20%.

Forecasting Assistance

Based on our actual results through Q1 and our original annual budget, help me build an updated forecast for the remaining three quarters. Here is what's changed:

- Revenue is tracking 5% above plan
- We delayed 3 engineering hires from Q1 to Q2 (savings now, cost later)
- A large customer gave 90-day churn notice ($200K ARR)
- Marketing spend is 15% under budget (open director role unfilled)
- Our largest vendor increased prices by 8% effective Q3

Recalculate the full-year forecast with these adjustments and highlight the changes from the original budget.

Scenario Planning

Build three scenarios for our 2027 financial plan:

Base case: Current growth rate continues, planned hiring, no major changes **Upside case:** We land 2 additional enterprise deals in the pipeline ($300K each), hiring stays on plan **Downside case:** Growth slows by 30%, we lose 2 more mid-market customers, we freeze hiring in Q3

For each scenario, show: revenue, EBITDA, cash position at year-end, and months of runway. Identify the trigger points — what signals should we watch that would tell us we're in the upside or downside scenario?

Expense Management

Expense Categorization

I have 500 credit card transactions from last month that need to be categorized for our accounting system. Here are the category options: Travel, Meals & Entertainment, Software & Subscriptions, Office Supplies, Professional Development, Marketing, Hardware, Shipping, Utilities, Miscellaneous.

Categorize each transaction. Flag any that are ambiguous and explain your reasoning. Also flag any that look unusual and might need review (duplicate charges, amounts that seem high for the category, etc.).

Vendor Spend Analysis

Here is our vendor payment data for the past 12 months. Analyze: 1. Top 20 vendors by total spend 2. Vendor spend trend — are any growing faster than our revenue? 3. Identify software subscriptions and their annual cost — are there overlaps or unused tools? 4. Flag vendors where we might have negotiation leverage (high spend, long relationship, multiple contracts) 5. Highlight any single-vendor dependencies that represent a risk

Financial Analysis

KPI Analysis

Here is our monthly financial and operational data for the past 24 months. Calculate and analyze these SaaS KPIs:

1. Monthly Recurring Revenue (MRR) and growth rate
2. Annual Recurring Revenue (ARR)
3. Net Revenue Retention (NRR)
4. Customer Acquisition Cost (CAC) — using sales and marketing spend
5. Lifetime Value (LTV) — using average revenue per customer and churn rate
6. LTV:CAC ratio
7. Payback period
8. Gross margin and trend
9. Burn rate and runway
10. Rule of 40 score

For each metric, tell me where we stand relative to industry benchmarks and what the trend suggests.

Investment Analysis

We're evaluating whether to build or buy a data analytics capability. Help me build the financial analysis:

Build option: - 3 data engineers at $160K loaded cost each - Data infrastructure: $50K/year - Development timeline: 6 months to MVP, 12 months to full capability - Risk: engineering time, opportunity cost of pulling engineers from product work

Buy option: - Vendor quote: $120K/year for enterprise license - Implementation: $40K one-time professional services - Timeline: 8 weeks to production - Risk: vendor dependency, potential price increases, customization limitations

Build a 3-year total cost of ownership comparison. Include both financial and non-financial factors. Make a recommendation.

Pricing Analysis

We're considering a price increase for our SaaS product. Current pricing is $50/user/month for our Pro plan. We're considering a 15% increase to $57.50/user/month.

Help me model the impact: 1. If we assume 5% of customers churn due to the price increase, what's the net revenue impact? 2. At what churn rate does the price increase become revenue-negative? 3. What is the impact on LTV and payback period? 4. How should we communicate the increase to minimize churn? 5. Should we grandfather existing customers? Model both scenarios.

Financial Communication

Investor Updates

Write a monthly investor update for our Series A investors. Key updates:

- MRR grew 8% to $380K
- Closed two enterprise deals (named logos if approved)
- Launched new analytics feature — early adoption looks strong
- Hired VP of Sales (starts April 1)
- Cash: $4.2M, 18 months runway at current burn
- Challenge: customer onboarding taking longer than expected, working on it

Tone: transparent, confident, concise. Investors appreciate brevity and honesty. Under 500 words.

Finance Team Communications

I need to send a message to all department heads about the Q3 budget review process. Include: - Timeline (submissions due by [date], reviews during [week], final budget approved by [date]) - What they need to submit (current-year actual + forecast, next-year request, headcount plan) - Template link - One new requirement this year: every new budget request needs a brief ROI justification - Offer to meet 1:1 with any department head who wants help with their submission

Tone: helpful, not bureaucratic. Finance is a partner, not the budget police.

Excel and Spreadsheet Assistance

Finance professionals live in spreadsheets, and AI is a strong spreadsheet assistant.

Formula Help

I need an Excel formula that: - Calculates the weighted average cost of capital (WACC) - Uses inputs from cells B2 (equity %), B3 (cost of equity), B4 (debt %), B5 (cost of debt), B6 (tax rate) - Shows me the formula and explains each component

Financial Model Review

I've uploaded my financial model for a new product launch. Review it for: 1. Formula errors or circular references 2. Assumptions that seem unreasonable 3. Missing costs or revenue streams 4. Sensitivity of the outcome to key assumptions 5. Suggestions for additional scenarios to model

Dashboard Design

I need to design a financial dashboard for our executive team. It should update monthly and show: - Revenue and growth metrics - Profitability metrics - Cash position and runway - Key operational metrics that drive financial performance

For each metric, recommend: the visualization type, the comparison (vs. budget, vs. prior year, vs. target), and the RAG thresholds that should trigger attention.

Compliance and Audit Support

Audit Preparation

We have our annual audit starting next month. Help me prepare: 1. A checklist of documents the auditors will typically request 2. A schedule of deadlines for providing each document 3. A brief for department heads on what the auditors may ask them 4. Common audit findings for companies our size and how to preemptively address them

Internal Controls Documentation

Document our internal controls for the revenue recognition process. Walk through: 1. How revenue is recognized (when, by whom, under what criteria) 2. Segregation of duties 3. Approval workflows 4. System controls 5. Reconciliation procedures 6. Exception handling

The Accuracy Imperative

What matters most in finance AI use is accuracy.

Every number in a financial document has consequences. A revenue figure feeds a board presentation that influences fundraising. An expense forecast drives a hiring decision. A cash projection determines whether the company can afford a new initiative.

AI gets numbers right most of the time, but "most of the time" is not good enough in finance. The standard I recommend:

AI drafts, you verify. Use AI to build structures, write narratives, identify patterns, and accelerate analysis. Then verify every calculation, check every formula, and confirm every figure against your source data.

Never present AI output without review. No financial document generated with AI assistance should reach your CFO, your board, your investors, or any external party without a thorough human review.

Trust the structure, verify the numbers. AI is excellent at building logical frameworks for financial analysis. It is occasionally wrong on specific calculations. Trust the approach, check the math.

Keep a record. When you use AI for financial work, note it in your work papers. Not because it is shameful, but because auditability requires knowing how a number was derived.

The finance professionals who use AI well are not the ones who trust it blindly. They are the ones who use it to work faster while holding the same rigorous standards they have always applied. The speed comes from AI. The accuracy comes from you.

Chapter 14: Legal and Compliance

The most important sentence in this chapter: AI is not a lawyer, and nothing in this chapter constitutes legal advice.

That disclaimer is not throat-clearing. It reflects a fundamental reality about AI and legal work that every business professional needs to understand. AI can help with legal-adjacent tasks — drafting, research, organization, preparation — but it cannot replace the judgment, liability, and professional obligation that come with actual legal counsel.

With that caveat firmly in place, here is how AI can genuinely help with legal and compliance work in a business context. Used correctly, it saves significant time on document preparation, research, and administrative overhead. Used incorrectly — by relying on it for legal conclusions without professional verification — it can create serious problems.

What AI Can Do for Legal Work

Draft standard documents. NDAs, simple contracts, terms of service, privacy policies, employment agreements. AI produces solid first drafts of standard legal documents based on widely available templates and conventions. These drafts are starting points for your legal counsel, not finished products.

Review and summarize contracts. Upload a contract and ask AI to summarize the key terms, identify unusual clauses, flag risks, or compare it to a previous version. This is one of the most practically useful legal applications of AI.

Research legal concepts. AI can explain legal concepts in plain language, identify relevant regulations, and provide general information about legal requirements. This helps you understand the landscape before consulting a lawyer.

Organize and manage compliance documentation. Tracking which policies exist, when they were last updated, and what compliance requirements they address.

Draft policies and procedures. Internal policies for topics like data handling, workplace conduct, AI usage, and information security.

What AI Cannot Do for Legal Work

Provide binding legal advice. AI's output is informational, not advisory. It cannot form an attorney-client relationship, and no one can rely on it as legal counsel.

Guarantee accuracy on jurisdiction-specific questions. Law varies by jurisdiction — what is true in California may not be true in Texas, and what is true in the US may not be true in the EU. AI may conflate jurisdictions or present outdated information as current.

Replace professional judgment on high-stakes matters. Litigation strategy, regulatory filings, M&A documentation, IP prosecution, employment law compliance — these require a licensed attorney who can be held accountable for their advice.

Stay current. Laws and regulations change frequently. AI's training data has a cutoff, and it may not reflect recent legislative changes, court rulings, or regulatory guidance.

Contract Review and Analysis

Contract review is where most business professionals interact with legal documents, and where AI delivers the most immediate value.

Quick Contract Summary

> I've uploaded a 20-page vendor contract. Summarize: 1. What we're buying and for how much 2. Contract term and renewal provisions 3. Payment terms 4. Service level commitments (SLAs) 5. Termination provisions — how and when can either party exit? 6. Liability and indemnification — who is responsible for what? 7. Data handling and privacy provisions 8. Any unusual or non-standard clauses that I should pay attention to

This turns a two-hour contract review into a ten-minute exercise. You still need your lawyer to review before signing, but you go into that conversation informed and with specific questions rather than asking them to explain the whole thing.

Contract Comparison

> I'm uploading two versions of our SaaS agreement: the version we signed last year and the renewal version the vendor just sent. Compare them and identify every change, no matter how small. Categorize the changes as: - **Substantive:** Changes that affect our obligations, costs, or rights - **Administrative:** Changes to dates, names, references - **Cosmetic:** Formatting or language changes with no substantive impact
>
> For substantive changes, explain what the change means in practical terms and flag anything that works against our interests.

Clause Analysis

> Review the limitation of liability clause in this contract and explain: 1. What does it actually mean in plain English? 2. What risks does it create for us? 3. How does it compare to a typical limitation of liability clause in a SaaS agreement? 4. What modifications should we request?

Contract Template Development

> Help me create a standard consulting services agreement template for our company. We regularly engage independent consultants for projects ranging from $5K to $100K.
>
> Include sections for: - Scope of work (placeholder for project-specific details) - Compensation and payment terms - Intellectual property assignment - Confidentiality and NDA provisions - Term and termination - Representations and warranties - Limitation of liability - Independent contractor status (important for tax/employment law) - Governing law (our state is [state])
>
> IMPORTANT: This template must be reviewed and approved by our legal counsel before use. Draft it as a starting point, not a final document.

Regulatory Research

AI is useful for getting a general read on regulatory requirements before consulting specialists.

Regulatory Landscape Overview

> Our company is expanding from the US into the European market. Give me an overview of the key regulatory considerations: 1. GDPR — what are our main obligations as a B2B SaaS company processing EU customer data? 2. Data residency — do we need to store EU data in the EU? 3. Cookie consent — what's required for our website? 4. Contract requirements — do we need Data Processing Agreements? 5. What certifications or audits might EU enterprise customers require? 6. Employment law — what's different if we hire employees in the EU?
>
> I know this is complex and jurisdiction-specific. Give me the overview so I can have an informed conversation with our legal counsel and outside EU counsel.

Industry-Specific Compliance

> We're in the healthcare industry and need to understand HIPAA requirements for our new patient portal. Outline: 1. What qualifies as Protected Health Information (PHI)? 2. What are the key HIPAA Security Rule requirements for a cloud-based portal? 3. Do we need a Business Associate Agreement (BAA) with our cloud hosting provider? 4. What are the breach notification requirements? 5. What are the penalties for non-compliance?
>
> I'll use this to prepare for a meeting with our healthcare compliance attorney.

AI-Specific Regulations

> Give me a current overview of AI regulations that affect business use of AI tools: 1. The EU AI Act — what requirements apply to businesses that use AI (not build it)? 2. US state-level AI regulations — which states have passed relevant laws? 3. FTC guidance on AI marketing claims and transparency 4. SEC guidance on AI disclosures for public

companies 5. Industry-specific AI guidelines (financial services, healthcare, employment)

Focus on what a business USER of AI tools needs to know, not what an AI developer needs to know.

Policy Drafting

Privacy Policy

Draft a privacy policy for our B2B SaaS platform. We collect: - Account information (name, email, company, role) - Usage data (feature usage, login history) - Integration data (whatever the customer connects via API) - Payment information (processed via Stripe, we don't store card numbers)

We use: - Google Analytics for website analytics - Intercom for customer support - HubSpot for marketing automation - AWS for hosting (US-East region)

We serve customers in the US and EU.

IMPORTANT: This must be reviewed by legal counsel before publication. Draft it as a starting point that covers the standard requirements.

Terms of Service

Draft terms of service for our SaaS platform. Key terms to include: - We provide the software on a subscription basis - Customer owns their data; we have a license to process it for service delivery - Our SLA commitment: 99.9% uptime - Acceptable use policy (no illegal activity, no abuse of the platform) - Intellectual property (our IP remains ours, customer content remains theirs) - Limitation of liability - Governing law - Dispute resolution (arbitration vs. litigation)

Again: legal counsel must review before publication.

Internal Compliance Policies

Help me draft an anti-bribery and anti-corruption policy for our company. We have international clients and partners. The policy should: 1. State our zero-tolerance position clearly 2. Define what constitutes a bribe, kickback, or improper payment 3. Address gifts and entertainment (establish reasonable thresholds) 4. Cover political contributions and charitable donations 5. Include a reporting mechanism (whistleblower protection) 6. Specify consequences for violations 7. Require annual training acknowledgment

Legal Document Management

Contract Tracking

I need to build a contract management system. We have approximately 200 active contracts across vendors, customers, and partners. Help me design: 1. A contract tracking spreadsheet with fields for: parties, type, value, start date, end date, renewal type (auto-renew vs. opt-in), notice period, owner, and key terms 2. An alert system for contracts approaching renewal (30/60/90 day notices) 3. A quarterly contract review agenda template 4. A checklist for contract renewal evaluation

Compliance Calendar

Create a compliance calendar for our company. We need to track: 1. Annual regulatory filings and deadlines 2. Insurance renewal dates 3. License and permit renewals 4. Required training (harassment prevention, security awareness, etc.) 5. Policy review dates (when each policy is due for update) 6. Audit schedules

Organize by month and include responsible parties and lead time needed for each item.

Working with Outside Counsel

AI helps you work more efficiently with your lawyers.

Preparing for Legal Consultations

I have a meeting with our employment attorney next week to discuss three issues: 1. We want to implement a non-compete agreement for senior employees 2. An employee has filed a disability accommodation request 3. We're unsure whether our independent contractors should be reclassified as employees

> For each issue, help me prepare: - Background summary to send the attorney in advance - Specific questions I should ask - Information and documents I should bring to the meeting - General context about the legal landscape (so I can have an informed discussion)

Summarizing Legal Advice

After receiving advice from counsel:

> Here are the notes from my meeting with our employment attorney. Summarize the advice into: 1. Action items with deadlines 2. Key decisions we need to make 3. Risks identified and recommended mitigations 4. A brief for our leadership team (translate legal advice into business language)

Intellectual Property

IP Inventory

> Help me create an IP inventory for our company. We need to track: - Trademarks (registered and common law) - Patents (filed and granted) - Copyrights (registered works) - Trade secrets (identified and protected) - Domain names - Software licenses (open source components in our product)
>
> For each category, create a tracking template with relevant fields (registration numbers, filing dates, renewal dates, jurisdictions, etc.)

Open Source Compliance

> We use the following open source libraries in our product: [list]. For each one, identify: 1. The license type 2. Key obligations (attribution, share-alike, patent grants) 3. Compatibility with our commercial license (proprietary SaaS) 4. Any restrictions on use 5. Flag any licenses that could be problematic (copyleft in a proprietary product)

The Liability Line

The most important principle, restated: AI in legal contexts is a productivity tool, not a decision-making tool.

The line is clear:

Appropriate: Using AI to draft a first version of a standard contract, then having your attorney review and finalize it. This saves your attorney time and saves you money.

Inappropriate: Using AI to draft a contract and signing it without legal review because "the AI said it was standard."

Appropriate: Using AI to research the general requirements of GDPR before meeting with your data privacy counsel, so you can have a more productive conversation.

Inappropriate: Using AI's explanation of GDPR to build your compliance program without involving qualified counsel.

Appropriate: Having AI summarize a complex legal document so you understand the key terms before your lawyer explains the nuances.

Inappropriate: Relying on AI's summary to make a legal decision without consulting a lawyer.

The professionals who use AI most effectively in legal contexts understand this line intuitively. AI makes you a better-prepared, more informed consumer of legal services. It does not make you a lawyer.

Think of it as having a very knowledgeable friend who happens to know a lot about law. You would listen to your friend's perspective. You would not let your friend represent you in court.

Use AI to prepare. Rely on professionals to advise. The combination saves time and money while preserving the rigor that legal work demands.

Part V: Strategy and Management

"Management is doing things right; leadership is doing the right things."

— Peter Drucker

Chapter 15: Project Management

Project management is the business function that ties everything else together. Every initiative, every product launch, every office move, every system migration requires planning, coordination, tracking, and communication. And project managers spend a disproportionate share of their time on the communication part: writing status reports, updating stakeholders, sending reminders, documenting decisions, and building the paper trail that keeps complex work on track.

AI excels at exactly these tasks. It does not replace the project manager's judgment, relationship management, or ability to navigate organizational complexity. But it dramatically cuts the administrative overhead that makes project management exhausting.

Project Planning

Project Charter

> I'm kicking off a project to migrate our company from Slack to Microsoft Teams. Create a project charter that includes:
>
> - Project purpose and business justification (we're consolidating on Microsoft 365 to reduce costs and complexity)
> - Scope: what's in and what's out
> - Key stakeholders and their roles
> - High-level timeline
> - Success criteria — how will we know this project succeeded?
> - Key risks and assumptions
> - Resource requirements
> - Approval section
>
> Context: 200 employees, currently using Slack (paid plan) and Microsoft 365 (with Teams but not adopted). Target completion: 90 days. Budget: $25K for implementation, training, and change management.

Work Breakdown Structure

> Break down the Slack-to-Teams migration into a work breakdown structure (WBS). Include:
>
> Phase 1: Planning and Setup Phase 2: Technical Migration Phase 3: Training and Change Management Phase 4: Cutover Phase 5: Post-Migration Support
>
> For each phase, list the specific tasks, estimated duration, dependencies, and responsible team (IT, HR, Communications, Department Leads).

Timeline and Milestones

> Based on the WBS, create a project timeline with: - Major milestones with target dates - Task dependencies (what must finish before what can start) - Critical path identification — which tasks, if delayed, would delay the entire project? - Buffer time recommendations for tasks with high uncertainty - A simple Gantt chart description I can build in my project management tool

Resource Planning

> For the Slack-to-Teams migration, create a resource plan: 1. Which team members need to be involved and for how many hours? 2. When are the peak resource demands? 3. Are there resource conflicts with other known projects? 4. What external resources might we need (consultants, Microsoft support, training facilitators)? 5. What is the total internal labor cost of this project?

Status Reporting

Status reports are the single most time-consuming recurring task for most project managers, and AI cuts the effort by 60 to 80 percent.

Weekly Status Report

> Here are my rough notes from this week on the Teams migration project:

- Finished technical assessment of Slack data (channels, integrations, bots)

- Found 14 Slack integrations that need Teams equivalents — 9 have direct replacements, 3 need workarounds, 2 have no equivalent (escalated to IT director)
- Training plan drafted, sent to HR for review
- Pilot group selected (15 people from Product team), starting next Monday
- Risk: the 2 integrations with no equivalent are used heavily by Engineering, could cause pushback
- Budget tracking: $4,200 spent of $25K budget
- Next week: pilot kickoff, begin building training materials, finalize communication plan

> Turn this into a professional status report with: - RAG status for each workstream (timeline, budget, scope, risk) - Executive summary (3 sentences) - Detailed update by workstream - Risks and issues table - Key decisions needed - Next week's priorities

Stakeholder-Specific Updates

Different stakeholders need different levels of detail.

> Take this week's status report and create three versions: 1. **Executive summary** (5 sentences) for the CTO — focus on timeline, budget, and risks 2. **Department head update** for all department heads — focus on what affects their teams, when they need to act, and what to communicate to their people 3. **Pilot group update** for the 15 people in the pilot — focus on what to expect next week, what they need to do, and where to give feedback

Risk Management

Risk Assessment

> For the Teams migration project, help me build a risk register. Identify the top 15 risks, and for each one: - Description - Likelihood (High/Medium/Low) - Impact (High/Medium/Low) - Risk score (likelihood x impact) - Mitigation strategy - Owner - Contingency plan if the risk materializes
>
> Include risks across categories: technical, organizational, change management, vendor, timeline, and budget.

Issue Escalation

> We've hit a significant issue on the Teams migration: the Engineering team is threatening to refuse the migration because two critical Slack integrations have no Teams equivalent. The integrations are connected to their CI/CD pipeline and are used dozens of times per day.
>
> Help me: 1. Draft an issue escalation document for the CTO 2. Propose three options for resolving the issue (with pros, cons, cost, and timeline for each) 3. Write a communication to the Engineering team lead that acknowledges the concern and proposes a path forward 4. Recommend which option I should advocate for and why

Meeting and Communication Management

Kickoff Meeting

> Design a project kickoff meeting for the Teams migration. Agenda for a 60-minute meeting with all stakeholders: - Project overview and objectives - Timeline and milestones - Roles and responsibilities - What this means for each department - How we'll communicate (status reports, escalation paths) - Q&A
>
> Include speaker notes and a pre-read document to send before the meeting.

Change Communication Plan

> Create a communication plan for the Teams migration. I need to communicate to 200 employees at different points during the project. Design: 1. Initial announcement (before any work starts — set expectations) 2. Department-specific briefings (what changes for each department) 3. Training announcements (dates, logistics, expectations) 4. Cutover communication (step-by-step what happens on migration day) 5. Post-migration support information (where to get help)
>
> For each communication, specify: timing, audience, channel, sender (who should it come from?), and key messages.

Decision Documentation

> Document the following decision for our project records:

Decision: We will keep Slack active for 30 days after Teams migration as a read-only archive, then deactivate it.

Format as a decision log entry: - Decision number and date - Decision statement - Context and rationale - Options considered and why they were rejected - Who made the decision - Who was consulted - Impact and implications - Review date (if applicable)

Agile and Sprint Management

For teams using agile methodologies:

Sprint Planning

Help me plan our next two-week sprint. Here is our backlog of items with story points: [list items]

Our team's average velocity is 34 points per sprint. We have one team member on vacation for the first week.

Recommend which items to include in the sprint, considering: 1. Dependencies between items 2. Reduced capacity due to the vacation 3. A good mix of feature work and tech debt 4. Our commitment to fixing the 3 high-priority bugs from last sprint

Sprint Retrospective

Facilitate a sprint retrospective. Here are the inputs from the team:

What went well: [list] What didn't go well: [list] Action items from last retro that we did/didn't complete: [list]

Organize these into themes, identify the top 3 issues to address, and propose specific, measurable action items for each. Each action item needs an owner and a deadline.

User Story Writing

Write user stories for the following feature: automated expense report approval.

The feature should allow managers to set rules for automatic approval (e.g., approve all expense reports under $100 from team members with no prior violations). Create: - 5-7 user stories using the "As a [user], I want [action], so that [benefit]" format - Acceptance criteria for each story - Estimated complexity (S/M/L) - Dependencies

Project Recovery

When projects go off track, AI helps diagnose and respond.

Project Health Assessment

> Our CRM implementation project is in trouble. It's 3 weeks behind schedule, 15% over budget, and stakeholder satisfaction is low. Here are the details: [provide current status, original plan, key issues]
>
> Analyze the situation: 1. What are the root causes of the schedule slip? 2. What are the root causes of the budget overrun? 3. Which issues are recoverable and which require a reset of expectations? 4. What are the options: compress schedule, reduce scope, add resources, extend timeline? 5. What should I recommend to the steering committee?

Recovery Plan

> Based on your analysis, draft a project recovery plan that includes: 1. Revised timeline with realistic dates 2. Scope adjustments (what to defer to phase 2) 3. Additional resources needed 4. Revised budget 5. Risk mitigation for the top 5 risks 6. Communication plan for stakeholders (how to deliver the bad news constructively) 7. Governance changes (more frequent checkpoints, escalation protocols)

Lessons Learned and Knowledge Management

Post-Project Review

> The Teams migration project is complete. Help me run a lessons learned exercise:
>
> 1. Create a lessons learned template with sections for: what went well, what went poorly, what we would do differently, process improvements for future projects
> 2. Draft a survey to send to all project participants
> 3. After I collect the responses, help me synthesize them into a lessons learned document that future project managers can reference

Project Playbook

> Based on our experience with the Teams migration, create a project playbook for future technology migration projects at our company. Include: 1. Standard project phases and gates 2. Role templates 3. Communication plan template 4. Risk categories to consider 5. Estimation guidelines (what to estimate and how) 6. Common pitfalls and how to avoid them 7. Checklists for key milestones

Tools and Integration

AI-Enhanced Project Management Tools

Several project management platforms now include AI features:

Notion AI helps generate project documents, summarize meeting notes, and create task descriptions within the Notion workspace.

Asana Intelligence offers AI-generated status updates, task prioritization, and workload recommendations.

Monday.com AI provides automated task generation from project descriptions and predictive analytics on project timelines.

Jira AI helps with sprint planning, story point estimation, and automated release notes.

These embedded AI features complement the general-purpose AI tools. Use the project management tool's AI for data-specific tasks (summarizing task history, predicting delays from past performance) and general-purpose AI for the thinking and writing tasks (status reports, stakeholder communications, risk analysis).

The PM's AI Workflow

A practical weekly workflow for an AI-enhanced project manager:

Monday: Use AI to generate the week's agenda from your project plan. Identify tasks that are due, overdue, or at risk. Draft kickoff communications for new work streams.

Daily: After standup or check-ins, paste your notes into AI and generate structured updates. Feed decisions and issues into your project documentation.

Wednesday (mid-week): Generate a mid-week status check. Are you on track for your weekly commitments? What needs attention?

Friday: Use AI to compile the weekly status report from your daily notes. Generate next week's priorities. Send stakeholder updates.

Monthly: Generate a project health dashboard. Run a risk review. Update the project plan with any scope or timeline changes.

This workflow means you spend your time managing the project — making decisions, solving problems, coordinating people — rather than writing about managing the project.

The Bottom Line

Project management is about keeping complex work organized, communicated, and on track. AI does not change what project management is. It changes how much time you spend on the administrative machinery versus the human work of leading, problem-solving, and making things happen.

The project manager who used to spend Friday afternoon writing status reports now spends it thinking about next week's challenges. The one who used to spend hours building project plans now has a solid first draft in minutes and refines it with their experience and judgment.

AI makes you a faster project manager. Your experience, relationships, and judgment make you a good one. The combination is formidable.

Chapter 16: Strategy and Decision-Making

Every chapter so far has been about using AI to do specific tasks faster and better. This one is different. It is about using AI to think better.

Strategy and decision-making are the highest-value activities in business. The CEO who makes three right strategic calls a year creates more value than a department of analysts working overtime. The manager who consistently makes good hiring, investment, and prioritization decisions outperforms the one who works harder but decides worse.

AI cannot make your strategic decisions for you. But it is an extraordinarily useful thinking partner — one that never gets tired, never forgets the question you asked an hour ago, has read more case studies than any human strategist, and will rigorously play devil's advocate when you ask it to.

AI as a Thinking Partner

The mental model that works best here is not "AI assistant" but "AI sparring partner." You are not delegating thinking to AI. You are thinking with AI.

In practice, that means using AI for:

- **Expanding your consideration set.** AI helps you surface options, angles, and factors you might not have considered on your own.
- **Stress-testing your reasoning.** AI pokes holes in your logic, names assumptions you are treating as facts, and challenges your conclusions.
- **Structuring messy problems.** When you have a tangle of considerations and cannot see a clear path, AI helps you organize the complexity.
- **Simulating perspectives.** AI can role-play different stakeholders, customers, or competitors to help you anticipate how others might respond to your decisions.

Strategic Analysis Frameworks

AI is fluent in the major strategy frameworks and can help you apply them to your specific situation.

SWOT Analysis

> Help me conduct a SWOT analysis for our company. We're a 150-person B2B SaaS company selling project management software to professional services firms. We've been in business for 6 years, have $12M ARR, and are growing at 25% year-over-year.
>
> Here's what I know: - Our product is loved by users (NPS of 62) - We're particularly strong in the consulting and accounting verticals - We're late to adding AI features compared to competitors - Our sales team is US-only but we're getting inbound interest from Europe - Monday.com and Asana are moving into our niche - The professional services market is consolidating
>
> Build a thorough SWOT analysis. Push beyond the obvious. Challenge my assumptions where warranted.

That last instruction is crucial. Without it, AI tends to produce a polite, surface-level SWOT. With it, you get something more honest and therefore more useful.

Porter's Five Forces

> Apply Porter's Five Forces analysis to the professional services project management software market. Be specific to our situation as a mid-market player:
>
> 1. Threat of new entrants — how easy is it for new competitors to enter?
> 2. Bargaining power of suppliers — who are our key suppliers and how much leverage do they have?
> 3. Bargaining power of buyers — how much leverage do our customers have?
> 4. Threat of substitutes — what alternatives exist beyond direct competitors?
> 5. Competitive rivalry — how intense is competition in our space?
>
> For each force, rate it (High/Medium/Low), explain why, and identify the implications for our strategy.

Strategic Options Evaluation

> We're considering three strategic options for the next 2 years:
>
> **Option A: Go deep in professional services.** Double down on our current vertical. Build specialized features for consulting firms, accounting firms, and law firms. Stay US-focused.
>
> **Option B: Go broad across verticals.** Build a more horizontal product that serves multiple industries. Invest in general-purpose features rather than vertical-specific ones. Stay US-focused.
>
> **Option C: Go international.** Keep our current product and vertical focus but expand into UK and EU markets. Invest in localization, compliance, and international sales.
>
> For each option, analyze: - Strategic rationale (why this makes sense) - Revenue potential (order of magnitude) - Required investment (people, money, time) - Key risks - What we would need to give up (opportunity cost) - Likelihood of success given our current capabilities
>
> Then give me your honest recommendation and explain your reasoning.

Decision Frameworks

The Decision Matrix

When you have a specific decision to make with multiple criteria:

> I need to choose a new CRM vendor. I've narrowed it to Salesforce, HubSpot, and Pipedrive. Help me build a decision matrix with weighted criteria:
>
> Criteria and my weightings: - Ease of use (25%) — our team is not technical - Integration with our existing tools (20%) — must work with Outlook, Slack, and our billing system - Scalability (15%) — we'll grow from 20 to 50+ salespeople in 2 years - Cost (20%) — budget is a real constraint - Reporting capabilities (10%) - Implementation time and complexity (10%)
>
> Research each vendor against these criteria. Score each on a 1-5 scale with justification. Calculate weighted scores. Make a recommendation.

Pre-Mortem Analysis

The pre-mortem is one of the most powerful strategic thinking tools, and AI is an ideal facilitator.

> We've decided to launch a new premium tier of our product at $200/user/month (current price is $80/user/month). I want you to conduct a pre-mortem.
>
> Imagine it's one year from now and this initiative has failed badly. Work backward and tell me: 1. What went wrong? Generate 10 specific, realistic failure scenarios. 2. For each scenario, how likely is it? (High/Medium/Low) 3. What early warning signs would we see if this failure mode was materializing? 4. What could we do now, before launch, to prevent or mitigate each failure mode?

Red Team Analysis

> I'm about to present our 2027 strategy to the board. Before I do, I want you to play the role of our most skeptical board member — someone who respects us but demands rigorous thinking and is not swayed by optimism.
>
> Here is the strategy: [paste strategy summary]
>
> Challenge every major assumption. Identify the weakest arguments. Ask the questions I'm hoping nobody asks. Point out where the evidence is thin or where I might be engaging in wishful thinking.
>
> Be direct. I need honesty, not validation.

Scenario Planning

Macro Scenario Planning

> Help me build three scenarios for how our industry (B2B SaaS for professional services) might evolve over the next 3-5 years:
>
> **Scenario 1: Continued growth** — the market continues on its current trajectory **Scenario 2: Consolidation** — large players acquire smaller ones, market concentrates **Scenario 3: Disruption** — AI fundamentally changes how professional services firms work, changing what they need from software

For each scenario: - What would trigger this scenario? - What would the market look like? - How would it affect our company specifically? - What should we be doing now to prepare for this scenario? - What leading indicators should we monitor?

Competitive Response Modeling

Our largest competitor just announced they're cutting prices by 30% and adding free AI features. Play out this scenario:

1. What is their likely strategic rationale?
2. How will the market react?
3. How will our current customers react?
4. What are our options? (Generate at least 5)
5. For each option, what are the short-term and long-term consequences?
6. What should we absolutely NOT do?
7. What should we do in the next 48 hours? Next 30 days? Next 90 days?

Decision Documentation

Good decision-making requires good documentation — not for bureaucracy, but because writing down your reasoning forces clarity and creates a record you can learn from.

Decision Record

Document this strategic decision:

We've decided to pursue Option A (go deep in professional services) rather than options B or C. Create a decision record:

1. Decision statement
2. Context and background
3. Options considered with brief rationale for each
4. Criteria used to evaluate options
5. Key factors that drove the decision
6. What we are explicitly choosing NOT to do (and why)
7. Key assumptions underlying this decision
8. Risks accepted
9. How and when we will revisit this decision

10. Stakeholders informed

Strategy Brief

> Convert our strategic planning discussion into a one-page strategy brief for the company. Everyone in the organization should understand:

- Where we are today (2-3 sentences)
- Where we are going (clear, specific vision for 2028)
- How we will get there (3-5 strategic priorities)
- What we are NOT doing (equally important)
- What this means for each department
- How we will measure success

Thinking Tools

Beyond formal frameworks, AI helps with the informal thinking that precedes good decisions.

Assumption Surfacing

> I'm about to make a significant hiring decision — bringing on a VP of Sales for $250K total comp. Before I commit, help me surface my assumptions:
>
> What am I assuming about: - The market conditions that justify this hire? - This person's ability to ramp and deliver? - Our product's readiness for the sales motion they'll run? - Our ability to support the team they'll build? - The timeline for this investment to pay off?
>
> For each assumption, rate how well-supported it is and what would happen if it turned out to be wrong.

Second-Order Effects

> We're considering implementing a 4-day work week (32 hours, same pay). Help me think through the second and third-order effects:
>
> First-order effects are obvious (employees work fewer hours, probably happier). What are the less obvious downstream consequences?

> Consider: productivity, hiring and retention, client expectations, competitive dynamics, cost implications, cultural effects, management challenges, and anything else you can think of.

Analogical Reasoning

> We're trying to decide whether to open-source the core of our product and monetize through enterprise features and support (the "open core" model).
>
> Give me 5 examples of companies that made this transition — some successfully, some unsuccessfully. For each, explain: - What they did and why - What went well - What went wrong - What the key lesson is for us

Group Decision-Making Support

AI helps facilitate group decision-making — not by making the decision, but by organizing the process.

Structured Debate

> Our leadership team is split on whether to pursue a partnership with a larger company or stay independent. There are valid arguments on both sides and we need to resolve this at our offsite.
>
> Design a structured decision-making process for 6 executives in a 2-hour session: 1. How should we frame the question? 2. What information should people review in advance? 3. What exercises or frameworks will help surface the best thinking? 4. How do we ensure minority viewpoints are heard? 5. How do we reach a decision without reverting to "the loudest person wins"?

Decision Synthesis

> We surveyed all 6 executives on the partnership question. Here are their written responses. Synthesize them: 1. Where is there agreement? 2. Where are the genuine disagreements (not just differences in emphasis)? 3. What are the underlying concerns driving the disagreements? 4. What additional information would resolve the disagreements? 5. What compromises or middle-ground positions might bridge the gaps?

The Limits of AI in Strategic Thinking

AI is a powerful thinking tool, but it has blind spots you need to be aware of.

AI lacks taste. It can analyze options against criteria, but it cannot feel which option is right the way an experienced leader can. Business instinct — the product of years of pattern recognition from lived experience — is something AI approximates but does not truly possess.

AI anchors on available information. It works with what you give it and what it learned in training. The crucial piece of context only you know — the CEO's personal motivation, the team's fragile morale, the customer relationship that defies logic — is not in the model.

AI can be too balanced. When you ask for analysis, AI tends to present a carefully balanced view. Sometimes you need not balance but a clear, opinionated perspective. When you want that, ask for it explicitly: "Give me your honest recommendation, not a balanced on-the-one-hand analysis."

AI cannot account for timing. Strategy is not just about what to do — it is about when. AI can analyze options but cannot feel whether the organization is ready for a major change, whether the market window is closing, or whether the moment is right for a bold move.

These limitations do not diminish AI's value as a thinking partner. They define how to use it: as one input among several, not the final word.

The Bottom Line

The most important decisions you make will never be delegated to AI. They will be made by you, drawing on your experience, judgment, values, and understanding of context that no model can replicate.

But the quality of those decisions will be better if you use AI to prepare. An executive who has stress-tested their strategy with a rigorous AI pre-mortem, systematically evaluated options through AI-facilitated frameworks, and surfaced their assumptions with AI's help will make better decisions than one relying solely on their own thinking.

AI does not make decisions. It improves the thinking that precedes decisions. In business, that might be the most valuable application of all.

Part VI: AI Platforms at Work

"The machine does not isolate man from the great problems of nature but plunges him more deeply into them."

— Antoine de Saint-Exupéry

Chapter 17: AI in Microsoft 365

If your organization runs on Microsoft 365, Microsoft Copilot is the AI integration you need to understand. Not because it is the best AI in every category — it is not — but because it lives inside the tools you already use every day. When AI is in Word while you are writing, in Excel while you are analyzing, in Outlook while you are emailing, and in Teams while you are meeting, the friction of adoption drops to near zero.

This chapter is a practical guide to using Copilot across the Microsoft 365 suite. I will tell you what works well, what does not, and how to get the most out of each application.

Understanding Microsoft Copilot

First, some distinctions. Microsoft uses the "Copilot" name for several different products, and the confusion is understandable. The lineup also moves fast — what follows reflects the May 2026 state.

Microsoft Copilot (free): The consumer AI assistant available in Windows and on the web. Useful for general questions but not integrated into the Office apps in any deep way.

Microsoft 365 Copilot Business ($18–21/user/month): For organizations up to 300 seats. Includes Copilot inside Word, Excel, PowerPoint, Outlook, Teams, and OneNote, plus Copilot Notebooks, Pages, and Cowork. Powered by GPT-5.5 with Smart, Quick Response, and Think Deeper modes. The standard choice for small and mid-sized businesses.

Microsoft 365 Copilot Enterprise ($30/user/month): The full enterprise integration. Adds enterprise-grade compliance, Microsoft Graph connectors, and integration with the broader Microsoft Foundry agent platform (the renamed and expanded Azure AI Foundry).

Microsoft 365 Copilot E7 Frontier Suite ($99/user/month, May 1, 2026): The premium tier. Bundles Copilot with Agent 365, the Entra Suite, advanced Purview compliance, and priority access to new agent capabilities. Aimed at organizations going all-in on agentic workflows.

Agent 365 ($15/user/month standalone): Microsoft's agent platform on its own, for organizations that want to deploy agents without the full Copilot suite.

The Word, Excel, and PowerPoint Agents — agentic versions of Copilot that can work across multiple steps and files — went generally available on April 22, 2026. They are included in all 365 Copilot tiers.

Organizational data access through Microsoft Graph is the key differentiator. When you ask Copilot in Microsoft 365 to "summarize the emails from Sarah about the Henderson project," it can actually do that because it has access to your inbox. A standalone AI tool cannot.

Copilot in Word

Drafting Documents

Copilot in Word can generate drafts from prompts or from existing content in your organization.

From a prompt: Open a new Word document, click the Copilot icon, and type:

> Draft a project proposal for upgrading our customer support platform. We're a 200-person company currently using a legacy ticketing system. The new platform should handle email, chat, and phone support with AI-powered ticket routing. Budget is approximately $75K for the first year.

Copilot generates a structured first draft. The quality is decent — it follows standard proposal conventions and produces a reasonable structure. You will want to add your specific data, examples, and organizational context.

From existing files: This is where Copilot's organizational integration shines:

> Create a project status report based on the project plan in /Teams/Henderson Project/Project Plan.xlsx and the meeting notes from last Tuesday's project standup.

Copilot pulls information from files in your SharePoint, OneDrive, and Teams channels and synthesizes them into a new document. This is genuinely useful and something standalone AI tools cannot do without manual copy-paste.

Editing and Rewriting

Select a passage in your document and ask Copilot to:

- "Make this more concise"
- "Rewrite this for a non-technical audience"
- "Make this more formal"
- "Expand this section with more detail"
- "Summarize this section in 3 bullet points"

These work well for routine editing. The rewrites are competent but can feel generic — you will usually want to review and adjust for your voice.

Summarizing Long Documents

Open a long document and ask Copilot to summarize it. This works particularly well for:

- Contracts and legal documents
- Policy manuals
- Research reports
- Meeting transcripts saved as Word documents

What works well: Extracting key points, identifying the main arguments, creating bullet-point summaries.

What does not work as well: Nuanced interpretation, understanding implicit meaning, handling documents with complex or contradictory content.

Copilot in Excel

Excel is where Copilot could be most transformative — and where the reality is most mixed.

What Works Well

Natural language data analysis:

"What are the top 5 products by revenue this quarter?" "Show me the monthly trend in customer acquisition cost." "Which region grew fastest year over year?"

Copilot answers these by analyzing your spreadsheet data and generating charts or tables. For basic questions about structured data, this is fast and convenient.

Formula generation:

"Create a formula to calculate the year-over-year growth rate for column C" "Write an INDEX MATCH formula to look up the price for the product name in cell A2" "Create a conditional formatting rule that highlights cells below the average"

Copilot generates Excel formulas from natural language. This is genuinely useful, especially for complex formulas whose syntax you would otherwise need to look up.

Creating charts:

"Create a bar chart comparing revenue by region" "Make a line chart showing monthly churn rate over the past 12 months"

Copilot generates charts directly in your spreadsheet. The charts are functional and appropriately formatted.

What Does Not Work as Well

Complex multi-step analysis. If your analysis requires combining data from multiple sheets, running conditional calculations, or following a specific methodology, Copilot often struggles. It works best with single-table analyses.

Pivot table creation. Copilot can create basic pivot tables, but complex pivot configurations with calculated fields and custom groupings often require manual setup.

Large datasets. Copilot can slow down or produce incomplete analyses with very large spreadsheets.

Accuracy verification. Critical: always verify Copilot's calculations. It occasionally misreads column headers, applies the wrong function, or produces plausible but incorrect results. Never include Copilot-generated numbers in a report without checking them.

Practical Excel Copilot Tips

- Keep your data well-structured: clear headers, consistent formatting, no merged cells
- Start with simple questions and build up to complex ones
- If Copilot's answer seems wrong, try rephrasing the question with more specific column references
- Use Copilot for formula generation even if you do not use it for analysis — this is its most reliable Excel feature

Copilot in PowerPoint

Creating Presentations

> "Create a presentation about our Q2 marketing strategy. Use information from the marketing plan document in /Marketing/2026 Plan.docx."

Copilot generates a multi-slide presentation with content pulled from the referenced document. It applies a template from your organization's PowerPoint themes and includes basic formatting.

Strengths: - Fast creation of a structured slide deck - Pulls content from existing documents - Follows your organization's branding template

Weaknesses: - Design quality is basic — you will want to refine layouts - Content tends toward bullet-point-heavy slides rather than visual storytelling - Image selection is limited to stock images or placeholders

Working with Existing Presentations

Copilot is more useful for enhancing existing presentations than creating them from scratch.

> "Add a summary slide at the end of this presentation" "Rewrite the speaker notes for slide 7 to be more conversational" "Add a slide comparing our product to Competitor X after slide 4" "Make this presentation shorter — consolidate into 10 slides"

Practical PowerPoint Copilot Tips

- Use Copilot to generate the content and structure, then manually refine the design
- The "create from document" feature works best with well-structured Word documents that have clear headings
- For high-stakes presentations, use Copilot for the first draft and then invest time in design polish

Copilot in Outlook

Copilot in Outlook is arguably the most consistently useful integration because email tasks are frequent, repetitive, and well-suited to AI.

Email Drafting

Click the Copilot icon in a new email or reply:

> "Write a reply thanking the vendor for their proposal and asking for a revised timeline. I need the deliverable by March 15, two weeks earlier than their proposal suggests."
>
> "Draft an email to the team announcing our new PTO policy. Key changes: unlimited PTO is being replaced with a 25-day allocation. Tone should be positive — explain the rationale (fairness and predictability)."

Email Summarization

For long email threads, Copilot can provide a quick summary:

> "Summarize this thread" "What are the action items from this conversation?" "What was decided about the budget?"

Particularly useful when you are added to an existing thread and need to get up to speed.

Email Coaching

> "Is this email too long? Suggest how to shorten it." "Check the tone of this email — is it too aggressive?" "Is there anything important I forgot to address?"

Practical Outlook Copilot Tips

- Copilot in Outlook works best for standard business emails — it tends to struggle with highly nuanced or politically sensitive communications
- Always review suggested replies before sending — Copilot occasionally misreads the context of a conversation
- Use it most aggressively for routine correspondence and most cautiously for sensitive or high-stakes emails

Copilot in Teams

Meeting Summaries

This is Copilot's strongest Teams feature. After a meeting (or during one, with the transcript running):

> "Summarize this meeting" "What were the key decisions?" "List all action items with owners" "What did Sarah say about the timeline?" "Were there any disagreements?"

Meeting summaries are genuinely good. They capture the substance of the conversation, identify decisions and action items, and attribute statements to the right speakers. For many organizations, this alone justifies the Copilot investment.

Chat Assistance

In Teams chat:

> "Catch me up on what happened in the #marketing channel today"
> "Summarize the discussion about the product launch"

Practical Teams Copilot Tips

- Enable transcription for all meetings where Copilot will be used — it works from the transcript
- Tell participants that the meeting is being transcribed
- Review the AI summary before distributing — it occasionally misattributes statements or misses context

- The "what did [person] say about [topic]" query is incredibly useful for long meetings

The Organizational Data Advantage

Microsoft 365 Copilot's biggest advantage over standalone AI tools is its access to your organizational data through Microsoft Graph. Copilot can:

- Search your emails for relevant context
- Reference documents in SharePoint and OneDrive
- Understand your meeting history and calendar
- Know your organizational relationships
- Pull information from across the Microsoft 365 ecosystem

This creates a fundamentally different experience. Ask a standalone AI to help you write a status report and you must provide all the context. Ask Copilot and it pulls context from your recent meetings, relevant files, and email threads.

The practical implication: Copilot gets more useful as your organization puts more of its work into the Microsoft 365 ecosystem.

Honest Assessment

Let me give you the unvarnished view after extensive use.

Copilot is most useful in: Teams (meeting summaries), Outlook (email), and Word (document drafting from organizational context).

Copilot is adequate in: Excel (basic analysis and formulas) and PowerPoint (content generation, not design).

Copilot's main limitation: Output quality is generally good but rarely excellent. For the highest-quality writing, analysis, or strategic thinking, standalone tools like Claude or ChatGPT still produce superior results. Copilot's advantage is convenience and organizational context, not raw capability.

The cost question: At $18–30/user/month on top of an existing Microsoft 365 business plan — or $99/user/month for the E7 Frontier Suite — Copilot is not cheap. For heavy Office users who live in Outlook, Word, and Teams all day, the time savings easily justify the cost. For light users who mainly use email and occasionally edit documents, the ROI is less clear.

My recommendation: start with a pilot group of 10 to 20 heavy Office users. Measure time savings over 60 days. Then decide whether to expand based on demonstrated value.

The Bottom Line

Microsoft Copilot's killer feature is not any single capability — it is the integration. AI that lives inside the tools you already use, with access to the data you are already working with, is categorically different from AI that requires a separate window and copy-paste.

For Microsoft 365 organizations, Copilot is not the best AI for any single task. But it is the most convenient AI for the tasks you do most often. In the real world of busy professionals, convenience wins.

Chapter 18: AI in Google Workspace

If your organization runs on Google Workspace, Gemini is your integrated AI companion. Like Copilot in Microsoft 365, Gemini's primary advantage is not that it is the most capable AI on the market — it is that it lives inside the tools you use all day. When AI is available in Gmail while you compose, in Docs while you write, in Sheets while you analyze, and in Meet while you converse, adoption becomes frictionless.

This chapter covers the practical reality of Gemini across Google Workspace — what works well, what is still maturing, and how to get the most from each integration.

Understanding Gemini in Workspace

Google's AI branding has evolved rapidly, so here is a quick map of the current (May 2026) landscape. The flagship model powering most of these surfaces is **Gemini 3.1 Pro**, with **Gemini 3 Flash** for lower-latency tasks and **Gemini 3.1 Pro Deep Think** for harder reasoning. The Workspace integrations are now branded as **Gemini Apps**.

Gemini (standalone): The AI assistant available at gemini.google.com, comparable to ChatGPT. Tiers: Free, Google AI Plus ($7.99/month), Google AI Pro ($19.99/month), and Google AI Ultra ($249.99/month).

Gemini Apps in Google Workspace: AI features integrated into Gmail, Docs, Sheets, Slides, and Meet. For business plans, Gemini Apps is now bundled into the standard Workspace tiers rather than sold as a separate add-on.

Gemini for Workspace Enterprise: Full integration with organizational data, enterprise security, and admin controls. Available as part of Workspace Enterprise plans.

The key distinction is between individual and organizational access. For business use, you want the Workspace integration, which includes data privacy commitments (on business and enterprise plans, Google does not use your Workspace data to train AI models) and administrative controls.

Gemini in Gmail

Email Drafting

Gemini in Gmail offers a "Help me write" feature when composing or replying to emails.

Click "Help me write" and describe what you want:

> "Write a professional reply accepting the meeting but suggesting Thursday instead of Wednesday. I have a conflict on Wednesday afternoon."
>
> "Draft an email to the team summarizing the decisions from today's budget meeting. Key decisions: we approved the new hire in engineering, deferred the office renovation to Q4, and increased the marketing budget by 12%."

The drafts are solid for standard business correspondence. After generation, you can use tone controls to adjust:

- **Formalize:** Makes the language more professional
- **Elaborate:** Adds more detail
- **Shorten:** Reduces length
- **More casual:** Makes the tone friendlier

Tone adjustments work in real time and help you quickly calibrate the message to your audience.

Email Summarization

For long emails or threads, Gemini offers a "Summarize this email" button. It produces a concise summary at the top capturing the key points.

This feature works best for: - Long update emails with multiple topics - Multi-person threads where you need to catch up - Newsletters and industry updates - Customer communications with detailed requirements

Smart Reply and Smart Compose

Google's earlier AI features — Smart Reply (suggested short responses) and Smart Compose (predictive text while typing) — still work alongside Gemini. Smart Compose has improved noticeably, predicting longer and more contextually appropriate phrases.

Practical Gmail Tips

- Gemini drafts are cleaner and less verbose than Copilot's Outlook equivalents, but they can feel generic
- The tone adjustment buttons are the most underappreciated feature — use them instead of manually rewriting
- For complex or sensitive emails, draft with Gemini and then edit carefully — it handles structure, you handle nuance
- Gemini cannot access emails it was not directly presented with — unlike Copilot, it does not proactively search your inbox for context (this is improving but remains a limitation)

Gemini in Google Docs

Drafting in Docs

The "Help me write" panel in Docs works like Gmail but for longer-form content.

> "Write a quarterly business review document for Q1 2026. Include sections for financial performance, customer metrics, product updates, team updates, and priorities for Q2."
>
> "Draft an employee handbook section on our remote work policy. We require 2 days in-office (Tuesday and Thursday) with flexible hours. Core hours are 10 AM to 3 PM."

Gemini generates content directly in your document, which you can edit, expand, or regenerate.

Editing and Rewriting

Select text in your document and use Gemini to:

- Summarize long sections

- Rewrite for a different audience
- Change tone (professional, casual, technical)
- Shorten or expand
- Translate to other languages

Document Summarization

Open a long Google Doc and ask Gemini to summarize it. This works well for:

- Meeting notes and transcripts
- Research documents
- Long proposals or reports
- Shared documents from collaborators

Collaboration Features

Gemini integrates with Google Docs' collaboration features. When multiple people are working on a document, Gemini can:

- Summarize changes since your last edit
- Identify sections that need your review
- Generate content based on comments and suggestions from collaborators

Practical Docs Tips

- Gemini in Docs produces content that flows naturally with your existing text — it reads what is already there and matches the style
- The summary feature is excellent for long collaborative documents where you need to quickly grasp the current state
- For best results, provide context in your prompt about the document's purpose and audience
- Gemini handles structured content (lists, tables, FAQs) better than unstructured prose

Gemini in Google Sheets

Data Analysis

Gemini brings conversational data analysis to Sheets. With your data open, you can ask:

> "What was our total revenue in March?" "Which product category grew the fastest?" "Create a chart showing monthly sales by region." "What's the average deal size for enterprise customers?"

Gemini analyzes the data and returns answers, sometimes with generated charts or highlighted cells.

Formula Generation

Like Copilot in Excel, Gemini can generate formulas from natural language:

> "Create a formula that calculates the commission at 8% of revenue for deals over $10,000 and 5% for deals under $10,000" "Write a VLOOKUP to match customer names from Sheet1 to their account managers in Sheet2" "Create a formula to calculate the number of business days between columns A and B"

Data Cleanup

> "Find and highlight duplicate entries in column B" "Identify rows where the email address format looks incorrect" "Flag any entries where the date is in the future"

Practical Sheets Tips

- Gemini in Sheets is most reliable for single-sheet analyses with clean data
- Formula generation is the most consistently useful feature – it handles complex formulas well
- Always verify calculations before relying on them for decisions
- Chart generation is quick but basic – you may want to refine formatting manually
- Your sheet needs clear, descriptive headers for Gemini to interpret correctly

Gemini in Google Slides

Creating Presentations

Gemini can generate presentations from prompts or from existing Google Docs.

> "Create a presentation about our Q2 marketing strategy. 10 slides."
>
> "Generate a slide deck from the product roadmap document in my Drive."

The generated slides include layouts, placeholder images, and structured content. They follow your organization's Slides theme if one is set.

Working with Existing Slides

Gemini can enhance presentations you have started:

> "Generate a speaker notes draft for each slide" "Create a summary slide for the end of this presentation" "Suggest an image for this slide about team collaboration"

Image Generation

Gemini can generate images directly for use in Slides. This is useful for:

- Conceptual illustrations
- Background images
- Custom visuals that stock photos cannot provide

Quality is sufficient for internal presentations but may not meet the bar for client-facing or executive decks.

Practical Slides Tips

- Gemini-generated slides are a reasonable starting point but always need design refinement
- The "create from document" feature works best with well-structured Docs that have clear headings
- Use Gemini for content and structure, then manually improve design, alignment, and visual hierarchy

- Speaker notes generation is surprisingly useful — it produces reasonable talking points you can customize

Gemini in Google Meet

Meeting Summaries

With Gemini enabled, Google Meet can provide:

- Real-time transcription during the meeting
- Post-meeting summaries with key points
- Action item extraction
- Searchable transcripts

The summary captures the substance of the discussion and organizes it into a structured format with decisions, action items, and key discussion points.

Take Notes for Me

"Take notes for me" generates meeting notes in a Google Doc automatically shared with participants. The notes include:

- Summary of the meeting
- Action items with suggested owners
- Key decisions
- Follow-up topics

Practical Meet Tips

- Enable "Take notes for me" at the start of the meeting, not partway through
- Tell participants that AI notes are being generated
- Review and edit the generated notes before relying on them
- Quality depends partly on audio — in-person meetings captured by a single laptop microphone produce less accurate transcripts than individual headsets on video calls
- Action item extraction is good but not perfect — verify that all action items were captured

Google Drive and Gemini

One of Gemini's strongest integrations is Google Drive. You can ask Gemini to work with your existing files:

> "Summarize the quarterly report from the Finance folder" "Find the most recent version of our customer presentation" "What does the employee handbook say about parental leave?"

This effectively turns Google Drive into a knowledge base that Gemini can search and synthesize. For organizations with extensive documentation in Drive, it is a significant productivity multiplier.

Practical Drive Tips

- Organize your Drive with clear folder structures and file naming conventions — Gemini finds well-organized files more easily
- Gemini respects your sharing permissions — it can only access files you have permission to view
- "Find and summarize" works best with text-based documents (Docs, PDFs) rather than spreadsheets

Gemini vs. Copilot: The Honest Comparison

Many readers are evaluating one against the other. Here is a direct comparison.

Where Gemini wins: - More intuitive interface — the "Help me write" prompts feel more natural - Better image generation capability - Google Drive integration for searching and summarizing files - Competitive pricing: Google AI Pro at $19.99/month on the consumer side, and Workspace Business plans bundling Gemini Apps without an add-on fee, against Microsoft 365 Copilot Business at $18–21/user/month - More natural email drafting in Gmail

Where Copilot wins: - Stronger Excel integration (Excel is more capable than Sheets for complex analysis, and Copilot leverages that) - Better Teams meeting integration (more mature feature set) - Deeper organizational data access through Microsoft Graph - Better PowerPoint integration for creating presentations from documents - More enterprise features (compliance, admin controls)

Where they are roughly equal: - Email drafting and summarization - Document creation and editing - Basic data analysis - Overall quality of AI output

Which One Should You Choose?

This is the wrong question for most organizations. The right question is: which productivity suite does your organization use? On Google Workspace, use Gemini. On Microsoft 365, use Copilot. The AI integration is good in both, and the integration advantage outweighs the marginal differences in capability.

If you are picking a productivity suite from scratch, the AI capabilities are now close enough that they should not be the deciding factor. Choose based on what your team prefers, your existing infrastructure, and your other business requirements.

Getting the Most from Gemini

Organizational Setup

If you are an admin rolling out Gemini for your organization:

1. **Start with a pilot group.** Choose 15 to 20 users across different departments. Run the pilot for 60 days.
2. **Provide basic training.** Most people underuse AI features because they do not know they exist. A 30-minute overview video and a one-page quick-start guide go a long way.
3. **Set expectations.** Gemini is a productivity tool, not a magic wand. Be realistic about what it can and cannot do.
4. **Establish guidelines.** What data is appropriate to discuss with Gemini? Which tasks need human review before finalization? Create clear guidelines before rollout.
5. **Measure results.** Track adoption rates and survey users monthly on time savings and satisfaction.

Individual Power User Tips

1. **Use Gemini in every app, every day.** The more you use it, the better you get at prompting, and the more time you save.
2. **Be specific in your prompts.** "Help me write an email" produces generic output. "Help me write a follow-up email to a client who is 30

days past due on their invoice, keeping a friendly but firm tone" produces something useful.

3. **Use the tone controls.** Faster than reprompting and usually good results.
4. **Combine with standalone Gemini.** For tasks that require more sophisticated reasoning or longer conversations, use the standalone interface at gemini.google.com rather than the in-app integration.

The Bottom Line

Gemini in Google Workspace follows the same principle as Copilot in Microsoft 365: AI that lives where you work is AI that gets used. The individual features are each modestly useful. The compound effect of using AI across every app, every day, is transformative.

For Google Workspace organizations, Gemini is not an optional add-on to evaluate someday. It is a productivity multiplier available now, and your competitors are already adopting it. The question is not whether to use it but how quickly you can get your team up and running.

Chapter 19: Building AI Workflows for Your Team

So far we have been talking about individual AI use — one person using one tool for one task. That is where everyone starts, and it delivers real value. But the next level of impact comes when you move from individual use to team workflows: repeatable, AI-powered processes that anyone on your team can follow to produce consistent, high-quality results.

This chapter is about building those workflows. Not in the "hire a developer and build an AI pipeline" sense — that is a different book. This is practical workflow design that a business professional can create and deploy using the tools we have already discussed.

What Is an AI Workflow?

An AI workflow is a documented, repeatable process that integrates AI at one or more steps. It specifies:

- What triggers the workflow (what task or event starts it)
- What inputs are needed (data, documents, context)
- What AI tool is used and what prompt is given
- What human review is required
- What the output looks like
- Where the output goes

The key word is "repeatable." A workflow is not you using AI creatively for a one-off. It is a standardized process anyone on your team can follow to get a consistent result.

A Simple Example

Here is a basic AI workflow for producing a weekly client status report:

1. **Trigger:** Every Friday at 2 PM

2. **Input:** Project management tool data (tasks completed, in progress, blocked), time tracking data, any notes from client meetings this week
3. **AI step:** Paste data into Claude with the prompt template: "Generate a client-ready weekly status report from these project notes. Format: Executive Summary, Completed This Week, In Progress, Next Week, Risks. Tone: professional, concise. Include specific metrics where available."
4. **Human review:** Project manager reviews for accuracy and adds context AI cannot know (client-specific sensitivities, relationship dynamics)
5. **Output:** Formatted status report in Google Docs
6. **Distribution:** Email to client by 4 PM Friday

This workflow takes a task that used to require 45 minutes of writing and reduces it to 15 minutes of review and editing. More important, it standardizes the output — every status report follows the same structure and quality level, regardless of which project manager writes it.

Designing Effective AI Workflows

Step 1: Identify the Right Tasks

Not every task benefits from being formalized into a workflow. The best candidates are:

- **Recurring:** Done at least weekly
- **Structured:** Follow a predictable pattern
- **Text-heavy:** Involve significant writing or analysis
- **Time-consuming:** Take enough time that automation is worth the setup
- **Consistent:** Should produce similar quality regardless of who does them

Here is a quick assessment:

> Help me identify AI workflow candidates for my marketing team. Here are the recurring tasks we do:

1. Weekly social media content creation (5 LinkedIn posts, daily Twitter)
2. Monthly newsletter writing (1,500 words)
3. Blog post writing (2 per week)

4. Campaign performance reporting (weekly)
5. Competitor monitoring (ad hoc, should be regular)
6. Content calendar planning (monthly)
7. Ad copy creation for new campaigns (as needed)
8. Customer testimonial formatting (as received)

For each task, rate its suitability for an AI workflow (High/Medium/Low) and explain why.

Step 2: Map the Current Process

Before adding AI, understand the existing process. How is this task done today? Where are the bottlenecks? Where is the quality inconsistent?

I want to build an AI workflow for our weekly campaign performance report. Here is how we currently do it:

1. Marketing analyst downloads data from Google Analytics, LinkedIn, and HubSpot (30 minutes)
2. Analyst copies data into a standard Excel template (15 minutes)
3. Analyst writes narrative commentary for each section (60 minutes)
4. Marketing director reviews and edits (20 minutes)
5. Analyst incorporates edits and formats final version (15 minutes)
6. Analyst distributes via email (5 minutes)

Total: approximately 2.5 hours

Where can AI have the most impact in this workflow?

Step 3: Design the AI-Enhanced Process

Now redesign the process with AI integrated at the right points.

For the campaign performance report, the AI-enhanced version might look like:

1. Analyst downloads data (30 minutes — unchanged, unless automated)
2. Analyst copies data into template (15 minutes — unchanged)
3. **AI generates narrative commentary** from a standardized prompt (5 minutes instead of 60)

4. Marketing director reviews AI-generated commentary and makes adjustments (10 minutes instead of 20, because the AI draft is more consistent)
5. Analyst makes final edits (5 minutes instead of 15)
6. Distribution (5 minutes — unchanged)

New total: approximately 1 hour and 10 minutes. Savings: 1 hour and 20 minutes per week, or roughly 70 hours per year from a single workflow.

Step 4: Build the Prompt Template

The prompt template is the heart of any AI workflow. It must be specific enough to produce consistent results and flexible enough to accommodate variations in the input data.

Here is the prompt template for our weekly campaign performance report:

```
WEEKLY CAMPAIGN PERFORMANCE REPORT PROMPT

You are a marketing analyst writing a weekly performance report
for the marketing director and VP of Marketing. Use the data
below to write the narrative commentary for each section.

Style guidelines:
- Professional but not stuffy
- Lead with the insight, not the number ("Email open rates
  improved 12% this week, driven by the new subject line
  testing program" — not "The number this week was 24.3%")
- Flag anything that is significantly above or below target
- Include specific recommendations where the data suggests
  an action
- Each section should be 3-5 sentences

Sections to write:
1. Overall Performance Summary (2-3 sentences)
2. Website Traffic & SEO
3. Email Marketing
4. Social Media
5. Paid Advertising
6. Content Performance
7. Lead Generation
8. Key Recommendations (3-5 bullet points)
```

```
This week's data:
[PASTE DATA HERE]

Targets for reference:
[PASTE TARGETS]

Notable context this week:
[ADD ANY CONTEXT: campaigns launched, seasonal factors,
events, etc.]
```

Step 5: Document and Train

A workflow is only useful if your team can follow it consistently.

> Create a workflow documentation page for our campaign performance report workflow. Include:
>
> 1. Purpose and overview
> 2. Who is responsible for each step
> 3. When each step happens (day and time)
> 4. Step-by-step instructions (including the exact prompt template)
> 5. What "good output" looks like (include an example)
> 6. Common issues and how to troubleshoot
> 7. Who to escalate to if something goes wrong
> 8. Version history (when the workflow was last updated)

Step 6: Iterate

No workflow is perfect on the first try. Run it for two to three weeks, gather feedback, and refine.

> After three weeks of using our campaign report workflow, here is the feedback: - The AI commentary on paid advertising is too generic — it doesn't account for our specific optimization strategies - The recommendations section is too conservative — the marketing director wants more bold suggestions - The email section keeps using jargon the VP doesn't understand
>
> Revise the prompt template to address these issues.

Common Business AI Workflows

Here are workflow designs for common business tasks you can adapt for your team.

Content Production Workflow

Trigger: Content calendar indicates a blog post is due **Input:** Topic, target keyword, audience, key message

Process: 1. Writer creates a brief with thesis, key points, and examples from experience 2. AI generates outline and first draft from brief 3. Writer reviews, adds personal examples and voice 4. AI assists with SEO optimization (meta tags, keyword placement) 5. Editor reviews final draft 6. Published

Prompt template: [Include the full prompt with placeholders for topic, keyword, audience, thesis, and key points]

Customer Onboarding Workflow

Trigger: New customer signs contract **Input:** Customer information, plan type, key contacts

Process: 1. AI generates personalized welcome email from template 2. AI creates customized onboarding checklist based on plan type 3. CS rep reviews and personalizes 4. AI generates training materials customized to their use case 5. CS rep delivers training 6. AI generates 30-day check-in agenda based on onboarding notes

Sales Proposal Workflow

Trigger: Opportunity reaches "proposal" stage in CRM **Input:** Discovery call notes, customer information, product fit analysis

Process: 1. AI generates proposal draft from discovery notes and template 2. Sales rep customizes with specific examples and pricing 3. AI reviews for consistency, tone, and completeness 4. Sales manager approves 5. Sales rep delivers

Monthly Board Report Workflow

Trigger: Fifth business day of each month **Input:** Financial data, departmental updates, KPIs

Process: 1. Finance provides data package 2. Department heads provide bullet-point updates 3. AI generates narrative sections from data and bullet points 4. AI compiles into board report format 5. CFO reviews financial sections 6. CEO reviews and adds strategic commentary 7. Board package distributed

Advanced Workflow Techniques

Chained Prompts

Some workflows benefit from multiple AI steps in sequence, where each step's output feeds the next.

Example: Market Research Workflow

Step 1 (Perplexity): "Research the top 5 trends in the cybersecurity market for 2026. Provide sources."

Step 2 (Claude): "Based on this research [paste Perplexity output], analyze which trends are most relevant to our product and why. Recommend three content topics that would position us as thought leaders."

Step 3 (ChatGPT): "Create detailed outlines for these three content pieces, optimized for our target audience of CISOs at mid-market companies."

Each step uses the tool best suited to the task, and each output builds on the previous one.

Quality Checkpoints

When accuracy matters, build in AI-powered quality checks.

> Before finalizing this report, review it against these quality criteria: 1. Every claim is supported by data from the input 2. Numbers in the narrative match numbers in the tables 3. Tone is consistent throughout 4. No speculative statements presented as facts 5. All sections are present and complete Flag any issues found.

Feedback Loops

Build in a mechanism for improving workflows over time.

> After each weekly report, the reviewer rates: quality (1-5), accuracy (1-5), and time to complete. Monthly, analyze the ratings and suggest prompt template adjustments to address any declining scores.

Scaling Workflows Across Teams

Once you have proven a workflow works for one team, scaling to others requires:

1. **Documentation:** Clear, step-by-step instructions that anyone can follow
2. **Templates:** Standardized prompt templates with clear placeholders
3. **Training:** A 30-minute walkthrough showing the workflow in action
4. **Support:** A point person for troubleshooting during the first two weeks
5. **Customization guidance:** How to adapt the workflow for different contexts while maintaining the core structure

> Design a training session for rolling out our AI-powered campaign reporting workflow to 4 additional marketing teams. Include: - Agenda (30 minutes) - Demo script - Hands-on exercise - Quick-reference card - FAQ document

Measuring Workflow Impact

Track these for each AI workflow:

- **Time savings:** Compare total process time before and after
- **Quality scores:** Subjective quality ratings from reviewers
- **Consistency:** Variation in output quality across team members
- **Adoption:** Percentage of team members using the workflow consistently
- **Error rate:** Frequency of issues caught in review

> Create a monthly workflow performance dashboard template that tracks these metrics across all our AI workflows. Include trend charts and highlight workflows that are improving or declining.

Common Pitfalls

Over-engineering. The best workflows are simple. If yours has twelve steps and three AI tools, it is probably too complex. Start simple, add complexity only when needed.

Under-reviewing. Every AI step needs a human review point. The temptation to skip review grows as you trust the AI more. Resist it — the one time you skip review is the time the AI produces something wrong.

Template drift. Over time, people modify prompt templates without documenting the changes. Maintain a single source of truth for each template and version-control it.

Not iterating. A workflow that never changes is a workflow that never improves. Schedule monthly reviews to refine based on feedback and results.

The Bottom Line

Individual AI use saves individual time. AI workflows save organizational time. That is the difference between one person being more productive and an entire team being more productive, consistently, every week.

Building AI workflows is not a technical project. It is a management decision. You are choosing to standardize and optimize the repetitive work that consumes your team's time, so they can focus their human capabilities on what matters most.

Start with one workflow. Prove the value. Then build the next. Within a few months, you will have an AI-enhanced operation that produces better work in less time — and you will wonder how you ever did it the old way.

Part VII: Adoption, Governance, and the Future

"Change is the law of life. And those who look only to the past or present are certain to miss the future."

— John F. Kennedy

Chapter 20: Managing AI Adoption

Rolling out AI tools to a team or organization is not a technology problem. It is a change management problem. The tools work fine. The challenge is getting people to use them, use them well, and use them consistently — while managing the anxieties, misconceptions, and organizational dynamics that accompany any significant change.

This chapter is for managers, department heads, and executives responsible for making AI adoption succeed beyond the early adopter phase. If you are trying to move your team from "a few people use ChatGPT sometimes" to "AI is a standard part of how we work," this is your playbook.

The Adoption Curve

AI adoption in organizations follows a predictable pattern. Understanding where your team is on this curve helps you choose the right interventions.

Phase 1: Curiosity (0–3 months). A few people experiment with AI tools on their own. They are excited but have no systematic approach. Usage is sporadic and mostly personal productivity.

Phase 2: Pockets of Value (3–6 months). Early adopters have found specific use cases that save real time. They tell colleagues, and interest grows. Adoption is uneven — some people are enthusiastic, others skeptical or anxious.

Phase 3: Intentional Adoption (6–12 months). Leadership decides to adopt AI tools formally. Licenses are purchased, training is provided, expectations are set. This is the phase where most organizations either succeed or stall.

Phase 4: Integration (12–18 months). AI becomes part of standard workflows. New hires are trained on AI-assisted processes. The question shifts from "should we use AI?" to "how do we use AI better?"

Phase 5: Optimization (18+ months). The organization continuously improves its AI processes, measures impact, and explores new applications. AI literacy becomes a core competency.

Most organizations reading this book are in Phase 1 or 2 and need a plan to move to Phase 3. Here is that plan.

The Adoption Plan

Step 1: Assess Your Starting Point

Before launching any initiative, understand where you are.

> Help me design a 10-question survey to assess our team's current AI readiness. I need to understand: 1. Current AI usage (who is using what, how often) 2. Comfort level with AI tools 3. Specific concerns or anxieties about AI 4. Tasks they think AI could help with 5. Training preferences (self-paced, instructor-led, peer mentoring)
>
> Keep it anonymous and under 5 minutes to complete.

The results will tell you who your early adopters are (they will become your champions), what concerns need addressing, and which use cases have the most demand.

Step 2: Define Your Objectives

What does success look like? Be specific.

Bad objective: "Increase AI adoption across the team." Good objective: "Within 90 days, 80% of the marketing team is using AI tools at least 3 times per week, with an average reported time savings of 5 hours per week per person."

> Help me define SMART objectives for our AI adoption initiative. Our context: - Team of 25 marketers - Currently, about 30% use AI regularly - Primary use cases: content creation, data analysis, email - Budget: $500/month for tools - Timeline: 90-day rollout

Step 3: Choose Your Tools

Based on earlier chapters, select tools that match your needs and budget. Keep it simple — start with one or two, not five.

For most teams, I recommend: - **One general-purpose AI tool** (ChatGPT Team or Claude Team) for thinking and writing - **One integrated tool** (Copilot or Gemini) if you are on a Microsoft or Google productivity suite - **Perplexity Pro** for research-heavy roles (optional)

Step 4: Run a Pilot

Do not roll out to the whole organization at once. Start with a pilot group of 10 to 15 people.

Pilot group selection criteria: - Mix of early adopters and open-minded skeptics (avoid all-enthusiasts — you need realistic adoption patterns) - Representation from different roles and levels - People willing to provide feedback - People whose work includes clear AI-applicable tasks

Pilot duration: 30 to 45 days

Pilot structure: - Week 1: Tool setup, basic training, first experiments - Weeks 2–3: Daily use, weekly check-ins, troubleshooting - Week 4: Measure results, collect feedback, document learnings - Week 5: Decision point — expand, adjust, or reconsider

Step 5: Train Effectively

Training is where most adoption initiatives succeed or fail.

What does not work: - A single one-hour training session with no follow-up - Generic "here is how AI works" presentations - Sending people a link to a tool and saying "try it out" - Training that focuses on features rather than use cases

What works:

Role-specific training. Marketers need different AI skills than salespeople or finance analysts. Customize training to show each role how AI applies to their actual tasks.

> Design a 45-minute training session for our marketing team. Structure: - 5 minutes: Why this matters (brief, no hype) - 10 minutes: Live demo of 3 high-value marketing use cases - 20 minutes: Hands-on exercise where each person uses AI for one of their actual tasks - 10 minutes: Tips, Q&A, and where to get help

Peer mentoring. Pair each participant with someone already comfortable with AI tools. The peer mentor answers questions, shares tips, and provides accountability.

Weekly tips. Send a weekly email or Slack message with one specific, practical AI tip. Keep it short — one use case, one prompt, one result.

> Write a series of 8 weekly "AI Tip of the Week" emails for our marketing team. Each one should: - Focus on one specific use case - Include the exact prompt to use - Show an example of the result - Take less than 2 minutes to read
>
> Make them practical and immediately actionable.

Office hours. Hold a weekly 30-minute drop-in where people can ask questions, share what they have tried, and troubleshoot. Less necessary over time but crucial in the first month.

Step 6: Address Concerns Directly

People have legitimate concerns about AI at work. Address them openly.

"Will AI take my job?" Address this directly in your kickoff communication. The honest answer: we are adopting AI to help you do your job better, not to replace you. AI handles the tedious parts so you can focus on what requires your expertise, creativity, and judgment. We are investing in these tools because we value your time and want you to spend it on high-impact work.

"Will management monitor my AI usage?" Be transparent about what you will and will not monitor. If you are tracking adoption metrics, say so. If you are not monitoring individual conversations, say that too. Ambiguity breeds anxiety.

"What if I use AI wrong and make a mistake?" Set clear guidelines (see below) and emphasize that human review is always required. Mistakes made while learning are expected and acceptable. Mistakes made by blindly trusting AI output without review are not.

"I'm not technical enough." AI tools in 2026 do not require technical skills. If you can write an email, you can use AI. Training will show you how — and your peer mentor will help you through the learning curve.

Step 7: Establish Guidelines

Every organization needs an AI usage policy. Chapter 21 covers privacy and security in depth, but here are the core elements for your adoption initiative:

> Draft an AI Usage Guidelines document for our team. Keep it to one page. Cover:

1. **Approved tools:** What tools we provide and support
2. **Data rules:** What can and cannot be shared with AI (confidential data, PII, trade secrets)
3. **Quality rules:** All AI-generated work must be reviewed by a human before use
4. **Attribution rules:** When and how to disclose AI use
5. **Security rules:** Use company-provided accounts, not personal accounts
6. **Expectations:** We encourage AI use — it's a tool, not a shortcut to skip thinking
7. **Support:** Where to get help, who to ask questions

Step 8: Measure and Communicate Results

Measurement sustains momentum and justifies continued investment.

What to measure: - Adoption rate (percentage of team using AI tools weekly) - Time savings (self-reported hours saved per week) - Quality indicators (relevant to your function) - Satisfaction (monthly pulse survey)

How to communicate: Share results openly. When someone saves significant time on a task using AI, celebrate it. When the team's aggregate time savings hits a milestone, broadcast it. Success stories are your most powerful adoption tool.

> Create a monthly "AI Impact Report" template for our team. Include: - Adoption metrics (usage rates, frequency) - Total hours saved across the team - Top use cases this month - Success story spotlight (one detailed example) - Tip of the month - Upcoming training or learning opportunities

Managing Resistance

Resistance to AI adoption is normal and usually rational. People resist change when they feel threatened, uninformed, or overwhelmed. Here is how to address the most common forms.

The Skeptic

"This is just another fad. We'll forget about it in six months."

Approach: Do not argue. Ask the skeptic to try AI for one specific task they find tedious. Let results do the persuading. Many of the strongest AI advocates were initially the most skeptical.

The Anxious

"I'm afraid AI will make my role less valuable."

Approach: Acknowledge the concern as legitimate. Point to specific examples of AI making similar roles more valuable, not less. Emphasize that AI literacy is a career asset.

The Perfectionist

"AI output isn't good enough. I can do it better myself."

Approach: They may be right — they probably can do it better themselves. The question is whether the time difference justifies the quality difference. Is a 90% quality first draft in 5 minutes better than a 95% quality first draft in 60 minutes? Usually, yes.

The Privacy Advocate

"I don't trust these tools with our data."

Approach: Valid concern; address it with specifics about your data protection measures. Refer them to Chapter 21 and your AI usage guidelines.

The Overenthusiast

"AI can do everything! Let's automate all the things!"

Approach: Channel the enthusiasm productively. Ask them to be a pilot participant or peer mentor. But temper expectations — AI is a tool, not a miracle. Quality still demands human judgment.

Organizational Structure for AI Adoption

Small Teams (5–20 people)

- One person serves as the "AI champion" — the go-to for questions and tips
- Weekly informal check-ins on what is working
- Shared prompt library in a team wiki or document
- Monthly review of what is saving time and what is not

Medium Organizations (20–200 people)

- Designate AI champions in each department (one per 10–15 people)
- Create a cross-functional "AI working group" that meets monthly
- Develop department-specific training and workflows
- Establish centralized guidelines with department-level customization
- Quarterly impact reporting

Large Organizations (200+ people)

- Dedicated AI enablement function (or responsibility within IT/digital transformation)
- Formal training curriculum with role-based tracks
- Centralized tool procurement and management
- Governance committee for AI policy
- Regular communication from leadership about AI strategy
- Integration with existing change management processes

The Role of Leadership

AI adoption starts at the top. If leadership does not visibly use and champion AI tools, the rest of the organization treats adoption as optional.

What leaders should do: - Use AI tools visibly — mention it in meetings: "I used Claude to draft the first version of this strategy doc and it saved me two hours." - Set expectations clearly — AI proficiency is part of professional development, not an optional hobby - Remove obstacles — ensure licenses are available, training is accessible, and time is allocated for learning - Celebrate wins — publicly recognize team members who find effective AI applications - Model responsible use — show that AI augments judgment rather than replacing it

The 90-Day Adoption Timeline

Here is a concrete timeline for a team-level AI rollout:

Weeks 1–2: Foundation - Conduct readiness survey - Select tools and purchase licenses - Draft guidelines and training materials - Identify pilot group and peer mentors

Weeks 3–4: Pilot Launch - Kickoff meeting with pilot group - Initial training session - Set up shared prompt library - Begin weekly office hours

Weeks 5–8: Pilot Execution - Pilot group uses tools daily - Weekly check-ins and troubleshooting - Collect time savings data - Document successful use cases

Weeks 9–10: Pilot Review - Analyze pilot results - Collect feedback - Adjust guidelines and training based on learnings - Prepare expansion plan

Weeks 11–12: Broader Rollout - Expand to full team - Deliver role-specific training - Assign peer mentors - Launch weekly tip series

Week 13: First Impact Report - Measure and communicate results - Celebrate early wins - Identify areas for improvement - Plan for the next quarter

The Bottom Line

AI adoption is not about technology. It is about people. The organizations that succeed treat AI adoption as a human change initiative — with clear communication, practical training, genuine concern for people's anxieties, and consistent support through the learning curve.

The tools are ready. The question is whether your organization has the management discipline to roll them out thoughtfully.

Done well, AI adoption transforms how your team works within a single quarter. Done poorly, it becomes another initiative everyone ignores. The difference is not the technology. It is the leadership.

Chapter 21: Privacy, Security, and Compliance

This is the chapter your legal team, IT department, and compliance officer need you to read. It is also the chapter that will keep you out of trouble — because the fastest way to derail an AI adoption initiative is a data incident that basic precautions would have prevented.

I am going to be direct about the risks. Not to scare you away from using AI — the benefits are real and significant, as the rest of this book demonstrates — but because managing these risks is a prerequisite for capturing those benefits responsibly.

The Core Risk: Where Does Your Data Go?

When you type something into an AI tool, your input travels to a server where the model processes it. The fundamental question: what happens to that input after the AI generates its response?

There are three possible answers, and they matter enormously for business use.

Option 1: Your Data Is Used for Training

Some AI providers use customer inputs to improve their models. Information you share could theoretically influence future model behavior. In the worst case, fragments of your data could appear in responses to other users.

Which tools do this? The defaults have shifted in the right direction over the last year, but training-on-input is still a live concern on consumer tiers when users opt in. As of May 2026: - **OpenAI** (ChatGPT Free, Plus, Pro): training on conversations is **off by default** on consumer plans (opt-in required) as of late 2025. Verify the current setting in your account. - **Anthropic** (Claude Free, Pro, Max): training on conversations is **off by default** on consumer plans (opt-in required) since August 28, 2025. Team, Enterprise, and API usage have always been excluded. - **Google** (Gemini consumer tiers): historically used conversations for training; check your current Activity controls.

Business implication: Even when training is off by default, employees can flip the setting accidentally — and "off by default" does not equal "no risk." Never share confidential business information — financial data, customer PII, trade secrets, legal matters, unreleased product information — with a consumer-tier AI tool. Use a business or enterprise tier with a contractual data-use commitment.

Option 2: Your Data Is Not Used for Training but Is Stored

Some AI tiers promise not to use your data for model training but still store your conversations for safety monitoring, abuse prevention, or troubleshooting.

Which tools do this? Most paid individual tiers (ChatGPT Plus, Claude Pro) fall into this category by default now, but data is still retained for a period for abuse monitoring. Verify current retention windows in each provider's terms — they evolve.

Business implication: Better than Option 1, but stored data can be reached in legal proceedings (subpoenas), data breaches, or compliance audits. For moderately sensitive business use, often acceptable. For highly sensitive data (legal privilege, M&A activity, personal health information), it may not be.

Option 3: Your Data Is Not Used for Training and Has Enhanced Protection

Enterprise AI tiers provide the strongest data protections: no training use, data encryption at rest and in transit, SOC 2 compliance, data residency options, and contractual commitments about data handling.

Which tools do this? ChatGPT Enterprise, Claude Enterprise, Microsoft 365 Copilot Enterprise and the E7 Frontier Suite (which inherit your M365 security and add Purview compliance, Entra Suite identity controls, and Microsoft Foundry agent governance), Agent 365, and Gemini for Workspace Enterprise.

Business implication: The tier you need for handling sensitive business data. Enterprise agreements typically include Data Processing Agreements (DPAs) that satisfy GDPR and other regulatory requirements.

Data Classification for AI

The most practical approach to AI data security is classification: decide which types of data belong on which AI tiers.

A Simple Three-Tier Framework

Green — Share Freely Data that is publicly available or has no confidentiality requirements. - Published content - General business questions ("How do I structure a marketing plan?") - Industry research queries - Editing and formatting requests on non-sensitive content - General strategy brainstorming without specific company details

Yellow — Share with Business-Tier Tools Only Data that is confidential but not regulated or legally sensitive. - Internal reports and financials (non-public) - Employee information (non-PII) - Customer data (anonymized or aggregated) - Product roadmap details - Competitive intelligence - Sales pipeline data

Red — Share Only with Enterprise-Tier Tools or Not at All Data subject to legal, regulatory, or contractual protections. - Personally identifiable information (PII) - Protected health information (PHI) - Financial records subject to SOX or similar regulations - Legal documents subject to attorney-client privilege - M&A or pre-announcement investor information - Customer data protected by contract (DPA/NDA) - Credentials, API keys, access tokens - Any data subject to GDPR, CCPA, HIPAA, or similar regulations

> Create a one-page data classification guide for AI use at our company. Use the Green/Yellow/Red framework above and include specific examples relevant to our business (B2B SaaS, 200 employees, US and EU customers).

Regulatory Considerations

GDPR (EU/UK)

If you process data on EU or UK residents, GDPR applies to your AI use.

Key requirements: - **Lawful basis:** You need a lawful basis for processing personal data through AI tools. Legitimate interest typically applies for internal business use, but document it. - **Data Processing Agreements:** If your AI provider processes personal data on your behalf, you need a DPA in place. Enterprise AI tiers provide these. - **Data transfer:** If your AI provider processes data outside the EU, you need appropriate safeguards (Standard Contractual Clauses, adequacy decisions, etc.). - **Data subject rights:** Individuals have the right to know how their data is processed, including by AI tools. - **Data minimization:** Share only the minimum personal data necessary for the task. - **Transparency:** If you use AI to make decisions that significantly affect individuals (like automated screening of job applications), you have specific obligations to inform and provide human review.

Practical advice: Use enterprise-tier tools with GDPR-compliant DPAs. Anonymize personal data before sharing with AI where possible. Document your lawful basis for processing. Conduct a Data Protection Impact Assessment (DPIA) if your AI use involves large-scale processing of personal data.

CCPA/CPRA (California)

If you process personal information on California residents, similar principles apply. The California Consumer Privacy Act and its amendment (CPRA) require:

- Disclosure of AI use in data processing
- Consumer opt-out rights for certain AI processing
- Reasonable security measures for personal information
- Data minimization and purpose limitation

HIPAA (Healthcare)

If you handle protected health information:

- AI tools used with PHI must be HIPAA-compliant with a Business Associate Agreement (BAA)
- Not all AI providers offer BAAs — verify before using
- De-identify data before sharing with AI wherever possible
- Maintain audit trails of AI interactions involving PHI

SOX (Public Companies)

If your company is subject to Sarbanes-Oxley:

- AI-generated financial reports need the same internal controls as manually prepared ones
- Document AI's role in financial reporting
- Ensure auditability of AI-assisted financial analyses

- Maintain appropriate segregation of duties even when using AI

Industry-Specific Regulations

Financial services, healthcare, legal, education, and government sectors all have specific regulations that may affect AI use. Before deploying AI in a regulated industry, consult with your compliance team and outside counsel.

Security Best Practices

Account Management

- **Use business accounts, not personal accounts.** Ensure all AI tool use happens through company-managed accounts with appropriate data protection.
- **Enforce SSO where available.** Enterprise AI tiers support Single Sign-On, which tightens access control and simplifies offboarding.
- **Apply the principle of least privilege.** Not everyone needs access to every tool or every capability level.
- **Disable data sharing and training options.** In account settings, confirm that data sharing for model improvement is turned off.

Data Handling

- **Never paste credentials, API keys, or passwords into AI tools.** Seems obvious; happens more often than you would think.
- **Anonymize data before sharing.** Replace customer names with "Customer A, B, C." Replace specific dollar amounts with ranges. Strip personally identifiable information. AI works with anonymized data just as effectively.
- **Be cautious with file uploads.** When you upload a spreadsheet or document, the entire contents are processed by the AI. Make sure the file contains nothing you would not want on the provider's servers.
- **Clear conversation history regularly.** Do not let months of business conversations accumulate in AI tools needlessly.

AI-Specific Threats

Prompt injection: Malicious inputs designed to make AI behave unexpectedly. Primarily a concern for organizations building AI-powered products, but worth being aware of. Do not paste untrusted content (like random documents from the internet) into AI tools that have access to sensitive systems.

Social engineering via AI: Bad actors can use AI to create convincing phishing emails, fake voice messages, and impersonation attacks. Train your team to be skeptical of unexpected requests, even if they sound perfectly natural — because AI-generated ones do.

Shadow AI: The biggest security risk in most organizations is not the AI tools they have sanctioned — it is the ones employees use without IT's knowledge. Free tools, browser extensions, and third-party AI features may have no data protection whatsoever. The best defense against shadow AI is providing good sanctioned tools so people do not need to go rogue.

Building Your AI Policy

Every organization needs a formal AI usage policy. Here is a framework:

Policy Components

1. **Purpose and scope:** Why we have this policy, who it applies to
2. **Approved tools:** Which AI tools are sanctioned for business use
3. **Data classification:** What data can be used with which tools (Green/Yellow/Red framework)
4. **Prohibited uses:** What is explicitly not allowed (sharing PII, using free tools for confidential data, etc.)
5. **Human review requirements:** When AI output must be reviewed by a human before use
6. **Disclosure and transparency:** When to disclose AI use to clients, partners, or the public
7. **Intellectual property:** Who owns AI-generated content, how it relates to company IP policies
8. **Incident reporting:** What to do if you accidentally share sensitive data with an AI tool

9. **Compliance integration:** How AI use relates to existing compliance obligations
10. **Training requirements:** What training is required before using AI tools

Sample Policy Language

> **Data Protection Rule:** Employees must not input confidential client data, personally identifiable information, protected health information, or data subject to regulatory protection into AI tools unless using an enterprise-tier tool with an approved Data Processing Agreement. When in doubt, anonymize the data before sharing or consult with IT.
>
> **Human Review Rule:** All AI-generated content intended for external distribution (client deliverables, marketing materials, legal documents, financial reports) must be reviewed and approved by a qualified human before distribution. This review must verify factual accuracy, appropriate tone, and compliance with applicable standards.
>
> **Incident Reporting Rule:** If you inadvertently share sensitive or protected data with an AI tool, report the incident to IT security within 24 hours using the standard incident reporting process. Early reporting enables rapid response and minimizes potential impact.

Third-Party AI Risk

When evaluating AI tools for business use, assess each vendor against these criteria:

> Create a vendor assessment checklist for evaluating AI tools for business use. Include:

1. Data handling: How is our data stored, processed, and deleted?
2. Training: Is our data used to train or improve models?
3. Security certifications: SOC 2, ISO 27001, etc.
4. Data residency: Where is data processed and stored?
5. Compliance: GDPR, CCPA, HIPAA, SOX compliance
6. Subprocessors: Who else handles our data?
7. Incident response: What is their breach notification process?
8. DPA availability: Do they offer a Data Processing Agreement?

9. Data retention: How long is data stored? Can we control retention?
10. Audit rights: Can we audit their data handling practices?

Practical Decision Matrix

A quick reference for busy professionals:

Data Type	Free AI	Paid Individual	Business Tier	Enterprise Tier
Public information	Yes	Yes	Yes	Yes
General business questions	Yes	Yes	Yes	Yes
Internal documents	No	Caution	Yes	Yes
Financial data	No	No	Caution	Yes
Customer PII	No	No	No	Yes (with DPA)
Regulated data (HIPAA, etc.)	No	No	No	Only with BAA
Legal privileged information	No	No	No	Consult counsel
Credentials /passwords	No	No	No	No

Staying Current

AI privacy and security evolves rapidly. New regulations, new product features, and new risks emerge regularly.

Stay informed by: - Following your AI providers' trust and safety pages for policy updates - Subscribing to IAPP (International Association of Privacy Professionals) updates - Reviewing your AI policy quarterly - Participating in industry groups focused on responsible AI use - Working with your legal and compliance teams to monitor regulatory changes

The Bottom Line

Privacy, security, and compliance are not obstacles to AI adoption — they enable it. An organization with clear policies, appropriate tool tiers, and well-trained employees can use AI confidently and aggressively. An organization that ignores these issues will eventually have an incident that sets back AI adoption by months or years.

The investment in doing this right is modest: choose the right tool tiers, write clear policies, train your people, review regularly. The cost of doing it wrong — regulatory fines, damage to client trust, data breaches, legal liability — is enormous.

Do the work upfront. Then use AI with confidence.

Chapter 22: The Ethical Business Use of AI

The previous chapter covered the legal and regulatory side of AI — what you must do to stay compliant. This chapter covers what you should do to stay ethical. The two overlap significantly, but they are not the same. Compliance is about meeting minimum requirements. Ethics is about doing right by your employees, customers, and the broader market even when the law does not require it.

Some readers will be tempted to skip this chapter. Ethics sounds abstract — like something for academics and policy teams, not for the marketing manager who needs to get a campaign out the door.

Here is the practical reality. Businesses that get AI ethics wrong suffer real consequences: reputational damage, customer backlash, employee distrust, and the kind of public relations incidents no amount of crisis communication can repair. Businesses that get it right build a durable competitive advantage: trust.

Transparency: The Non-Negotiable

The single most important ethical principle for business AI use is transparency. Your customers, employees, and partners deserve to know when they are interacting with AI-generated content, AI-driven decisions, or AI-assisted processes.

This does not mean slapping a disclaimer on every email you drafted with AI assistance. That would be impractical and unnecessary. It does mean being honest in the situations where it matters.

When Disclosure Matters

Customer-facing decisions. If AI is influencing decisions about pricing, credit, service levels, or access to products, customers have a right to know. This is not just ethical — in many jurisdictions, it is increasingly a legal requirement. Even where it is not mandated, transparency about AI-driven decisions builds trust and gives customers a meaningful way to seek review.

Published content. If your company publishes articles, reports, whitepapers, or thought leadership that is substantially AI-generated, disclose it. You do not need to identify which sentences came from AI and which came from a human. A simple disclosure that AI tools were used in the creation process is enough. Your audience can then decide how much weight to give the content.

Hiring and personnel decisions. If you are using AI to screen resumes, evaluate candidates, or inform promotion decisions, the people affected need to know. Both ethical obligations and legal requirements are evolving rapidly here, and the trend is clearly toward more transparency, not less.

Customer service interactions. If a customer is chatting with a bot, they should know it is a bot. The technology is good enough now that some customers genuinely cannot tell the difference, which makes disclosure more important, not less. People communicate differently when they know they are talking to a machine, and they have a right to make that choice.

When Disclosure Is Less Critical

Internal productivity use. If you use AI to draft an internal memo, analyze a spreadsheet, or brainstorm ideas in your own workflow, you generally do not need to disclose this to anyone. AI is a tool, like spell check or a calculator. Nobody discloses that they used Excel's SUM function in their budget analysis.

Routine drafting assistance. Using AI to write emails, meeting agendas, or status updates falls into personal productivity. The output is still yours — you reviewed it, edited it, and sent it under your name.

The dividing line is influence and attribution. If someone might make a different decision knowing AI was involved, disclose. If the AI was simply helping you do your own work more efficiently, use your judgment.

Bias: The Risk You Cannot See

AI models are trained on data generated by humans, and humans are biased. AI systems can therefore perpetuate, amplify, and sometimes introduce biases related to gender, race, age, disability, socioeconomic status, and other characteristics.

For business use, this is not a theoretical concern. It is a practical one with real-world consequences.

Where Bias Shows Up in Business AI

Hiring. AI resume screening tools have shown bias against certain names, educational backgrounds, and career patterns that correlate with protected characteristics. Amazon famously scrapped an AI recruiting tool after discovering it penalized resumes that included the word "women's" — as in "women's chess club" or "women's college."

Marketing. AI-generated ad copy and targeting can reflect and reinforce stereotypes. Ask an AI to generate images of "a CEO" and count how many are white men. Ask it to write a job description for a nurse and notice the pronouns. These biases in AI output become your company's biases the moment you publish them.

Customer service. AI systems that route, prioritize, or respond to customer inquiries can treat different customer segments differently based on patterns in training data. If your AI customer service tool delivers faster, more helpful responses to customers in affluent zip codes, that is your company's bias, not the AI's.

Financial decisions. AI models used for credit scoring, pricing, insurance underwriting, or fraud detection can encode historical discrimination. If past lending decisions were biased, an AI trained on that data will replicate those biases with mathematical precision.

Performance evaluation. Using AI to analyze employee performance data can amplify existing biases in how performance is measured and rewarded. If your performance data reflects historical inequities in opportunity, AI analysis will present those inequities as objective findings.

How to Mitigate Bias

Audit your outputs. Periodically review AI-generated content, decisions, and recommendations for patterns that suggest bias. This does not require sophisticated statistical analysis — often, looking at the outputs with fresh eyes is enough to spot problems.

Diversify your prompts. When generating content that involves people — case studies, examples, images, scenarios — explicitly instruct the AI to include diverse representation. Left to its defaults, AI reproduces the demographic patterns of its training data, which skew toward certain groups.

Use AI to check AI. One effective technique is a second AI review pass that specifically looks for bias.

> Review this job description for any language that might discourage applications from women, minorities, people with disabilities, or older workers. Flag specific phrases and suggest alternatives.

Maintain human oversight for high-stakes decisions. For decisions that significantly affect people — hiring, firing, credit, pricing, service access — AI should inform but not decide. A human with the authority and context to override AI recommendations should always be in the loop.

Document your approach. Keep records of what AI tools you use, what decisions they influence, and what bias mitigation steps you have taken. This documentation protects you legally and helps you improve over time.

Attribution and Intellectual Property

When you use AI to generate content, who owns it? This question is still being settled in courts and legislatures around the world, but businesses need practical guidance now.

The Current Legal Landscape

As of early 2026, the general consensus in the United States is that purely AI-generated content — created entirely by AI with no meaningful human creative input — is not eligible for copyright protection. The U.S. Copyright Office has been clear on this point.

Content that involves substantial human creativity — where AI is used as a tool but a human makes meaningful creative decisions about selection, arrangement, and expression — is generally copyrightable by the human author.

For business purposes, the way you use AI matters. If you prompt an AI to "write a blog post about supply chain management" and publish the result unchanged, your copyright claim is weak. If you use AI to generate a draft, then substantially edit, reorganize, add original insights, and shape it into something that reflects your expertise and perspective, your claim is much stronger.

Practical Guidelines for Attribution

Do not pass off AI-generated work as original human creation in contexts where the distinction matters. If you are submitting a whitepaper to a conference, a report to a regulator, or content to a publication with policies about AI use, disclose honestly.

Do not use AI to generate content that infringes on others' work. AI models are trained on existing content and can sometimes produce outputs that closely resemble specific copyrighted works. If AI-generated content looks suspiciously similar to something you have read before, investigate before publishing.

Establish a company policy on AI attribution. Specify when disclosure is required, what form it takes, and who is responsible for compliance. Make it simple enough that people actually follow it.

Be especially careful with AI-generated images. Visual AI tools like DALL-E, Midjourney, and others create images based on training data that includes copyrighted artwork. The legal landscape here is particularly unsettled, and some stock photo services and publications have already banned AI-generated images. Know the policies of every platform where you publish visual content.

Using AI on Other People's Data

When you upload customer data, employee information, or partner data to an AI tool, you are making decisions about other people's information. That responsibility goes beyond legal compliance.

The Ethical Standard

The ethical standard is straightforward: use other people's data in ways they would reasonably expect and consent to if asked.

Your customers gave you their data to receive your product or service. They did not give it to you to upload to a third-party AI tool for analysis. Your employees share performance data as part of the employment relationship. They did not consent to having it processed by an AI system to make promotion decisions.

This does not mean you cannot use AI with this data. It means you need to be thoughtful.

Anonymize where possible. If you are analyzing customer feedback trends, you do not need individual names and account numbers in the prompt. Strip identifying information before uploading.

Use enterprise-tier tools for sensitive data. As discussed in Chapter 21, enterprise AI tiers offer stronger data protections. If you are processing other people's data, you owe them the protection of the right tier.

Consider the "newspaper test." Before uploading someone's data to an AI tool, ask yourself: if this appeared on the front page of a newspaper — "Company uploads customer data to AI chatbot" — would you be comfortable explaining your reasoning? If not, reconsider.

The Responsibility Question

When AI contributes to a business decision that turns out badly, who is responsible? The AI provider? The person who used the AI? The manager who approved the decision? The company?

The answer is clear, even if some people wish it were not: your organization is responsible for decisions made using AI tools, just as you are responsible for decisions made using spreadsheets, consultants, or any other resource.

AI is a tool. Tools do not bear responsibility. People and organizations do.

What This Means in Practice

Never use "the AI said so" as a justification. If you make a business decision based on AI analysis and that decision turns out wrong, the fact that AI was involved does not reduce your accountability. You chose to use the tool, you chose to act on its output, and the consequences are yours.

Build review processes. For any AI-assisted process with significant business impact, build in a human review step. Not a rubber-stamp review — a genuine evaluation by someone with the expertise and authority to override the AI's recommendation.

Maintain records. Document what AI tools were used, what inputs were provided, what outputs were generated, and what human review occurred. This protects you in disputes and helps you improve your processes over time.

Train your people. Make sure everyone using AI tools understands they are responsible for the outputs they act on. AI is not a shield against accountability — it is a tool that requires judgment to use well.

Competitive Ethics

AI creates new opportunities for competitive intelligence, and not all of those opportunities are ethical to pursue.

Using AI to analyze public information about competitors is fine. Competitor websites, published financials, press releases, patent filings, job postings — all public information. Using AI to analyze it quickly is no different from having an analyst do the same work manually.

Using AI to scrape, impersonate, or deceive is not fine. Do not use AI to generate fake reviews of competitors. Do not use AI to impersonate competitor employees. Do not use AI to create misleading content designed to confuse a competitor's customers. These were unethical before AI, and the efficiency AI brings does not make them less so.

Using AI-generated content to manipulate markets is illegal and unethical. Creating fake news articles, fabricated analyst reports, or deceptive social media campaigns with AI tools is fraud, regardless of how convincing the output is.

The ethical standard for competitive AI use is the same standard that has always applied: compete on the merits of your product and service, not on your ability to deceive.

Building an Ethical AI Culture

Ethics cannot be outsourced to a policy document. It has to be embedded in how your organization thinks about AI every day.

Five Steps to an Ethical AI Culture

1. Lead by example. If leadership uses AI transparently, discloses AI assistance where appropriate, and takes bias mitigation seriously, the rest of the organization will follow. If leadership treats ethics as a box to check, everyone else will too.

2. Create safe channels for raising concerns. People need to be able to say "I think this AI use case might be problematic" without fear of being dismissed as obstructionist. Some of the biggest corporate AI mistakes could have been prevented if someone lower in the organization had felt comfortable raising a flag.

3. Include ethics in AI training. When you train your team on AI tools, do not just cover the how — cover the should. Give people real scenarios and have them think through the ethical dimensions.

> I'm developing AI ethics training for our team. Create 5 realistic business scenarios where AI use raises ethical questions. For each scenario, provide: - The business situation - The AI use being considered - The ethical concerns involved - A recommended course of action - The reasoning behind the recommendation
>
> Make these specific to a mid-size B2B company. Avoid obvious cases — focus on situations where the right answer requires real thought.

4. Review regularly. AI capabilities change, norms evolve, and new use cases emerge. Review your ethical guidelines at least annually and update as needed.

5. Accept that mistakes will happen. No policy or training program will prevent every ethical misstep. What matters is how quickly you spot problems, how honestly you address them, and how effectively you prevent recurrence. A culture that punishes all mistakes drives them underground. A culture that learns from mistakes gets better over time.

The Bottom Line

The ethical use of AI in business is not complicated in principle. Be transparent when AI is involved. Watch for bias and take active steps to mitigate it. Respect other people's data. Take responsibility for AI-assisted decisions. Compete honestly.

It gets challenging in the gray areas — where the right answer is not obvious, where business incentives push one way and ethical considerations push the other. For those situations, there is no substitute for good judgment, honest conversation, and a genuine commitment to doing right by the people your business serves.

The companies that will thrive in the AI era are not the ones that adopt AI fastest. They are the ones that adopt it wisely — capturing the benefits while maintaining the trust of their customers, employees, and communities.

Ethics is not a constraint on your AI strategy. It is a foundation of it.

Chapter 23: Future-Proofing Your Business AI Strategy

This is the chapter I have been most careful about writing. Not because the topic is unimportant — it is arguably the most important in the book — but because the history of technology predictions is a graveyard of confident claims that aged poorly within months.

I am not going to tell you exactly what AI will look like in 2028 or 2030. Nobody knows. What I can do is identify the trends already underway, separate likely developments from speculative ones, and — most importantly — help you build an AI strategy that will serve your business regardless of which specific predictions come true.

That is what future-proofing actually means. Not predicting the future. Building the capacity to adapt to it.

What Is Clearly Coming

Some AI developments are not predictions — they are trajectories already in motion. The technology exists, market demand is clear, and the only question is timing and implementation details.

AI Agents That Take Action

In 2026, most business AI operates in a familiar pattern: you give it a task, it produces an output, you review and act on that output. The next phase — already emerging — is AI that takes sequences of actions on your behalf.

Imagine telling your AI assistant: "Book a meeting with the three highest-priority prospects from this week's leads, propose times that work around my existing calendar, send personalized outreach based on their company profiles, and add the meetings to our CRM with the appropriate pipeline stage."

Today, you would have to break that into six or seven separate tasks across multiple tools. Agentic AI will handle the full sequence, checking in at decision points but handling the routine steps autonomously.

What this means for your business: The teams that benefit most from agentic AI are the ones that have already documented their workflows clearly. If you know what your processes are — the steps, the decision criteria, the exceptions — you are ready to hand them to AI agents. If your workflows exist only in people's heads, you have work to do before agents can help.

> Help me document our lead qualification process as a step-by-step workflow, including decision criteria at each stage and the specific actions that need to be taken. Format it so that it could eventually be used as instructions for an AI agent.

Deeper Integration with Business Software

The AI-in-your-toolbar model (Copilot in Office, Gemini in Workspace) is just the beginning. The next wave is AI genuinely integrated into your business systems — your CRM, ERP, HR platform, project management tool, and financial systems — with the ability to read data across systems and take coordinated action.

Salesforce, HubSpot, Workday, ServiceNow, and other major enterprise platforms are all building AI capabilities that go far beyond chatbots. These are systems that understand your business data in context and can act on it.

What this means for your business: Your choice of business software platforms is increasingly an AI strategy decision. When evaluating new tools or renewing contracts, assess the vendor's AI roadmap alongside traditional feature comparisons. The platform with the best AI integration will deliver compounding value over time.

Specialized Industry Models

The general-purpose AI models — ChatGPT, Claude, Gemini — are extraordinarily capable, but they are generalists. The market is moving toward specialized models trained on industry-specific data: legal AI that understands case law and regulatory frameworks at depth, financial AI that can reason about complex instruments and compliance requirements, healthcare AI that speaks the language of clinical practice.

These specialized models will not replace general-purpose AI for most business tasks. But for industry-specific work — where general AI sometimes gets the nuances wrong — they will be significantly better.

What this means for your business: Keep an eye on AI tools emerging in your industry. The first generation is already available in legal, finance, healthcare, and real estate. They are often worth the premium over general-purpose tools for domain-specific tasks.

Multimodal AI Gets Practical

Current multimodal capabilities — uploading images, reading documents, analyzing charts — are useful but still somewhat limited. The trajectory is toward AI that works seamlessly across text, images, video, audio, and structured data in a single workflow.

Practical business applications: AI that watches a product demonstration video and generates sales collateral from it, AI that analyzes a physical space from photographs and produces facility management plans, AI that listens to customer calls and updates your CRM in real time with sentiment analysis and action items.

What this means for your business: Start thinking beyond text. Many of the most valuable AI applications in the next two to three years will involve non-text inputs. If your business generates video, audio, or visual content, assess how AI could process and leverage those assets.

Real-Time AI Collaboration

The current model of AI as a separate tool you switch to — opening ChatGPT in a browser tab, launching Copilot in Word — is giving way to AI as a constant, ambient presence in your work. Think of it less as a tool you use and more as a colleague who can see your screen and offers help when it is relevant.

Early versions are already appearing: AI that suggests edits as you type, AI that monitors your inbox and flags messages needing attention, AI that notices patterns in your calendar and suggests optimizations.

What this means for your business: The value of AI will increasingly come not from deliberate, prompted interactions but from ambient assistance that reduces friction throughout the workday. When evaluating AI tools, consider how naturally they integrate into existing workflows rather than how impressive their standalone capabilities are.

What Is Likely but Uncertain

These developments are probable, but the timing and form factor are less clear.

AI-to-AI Communication

As AI agents become more capable, businesses will start having their AI systems communicate directly with their customers' and partners' AI systems. Your procurement AI talks to a supplier's sales AI. Your scheduling AI negotiates meeting times with a client's scheduling AI. Your contract AI exchanges redlines with a counterparty's contract AI.

This sounds futuristic, but the technical foundations exist today. The questions are standards and trust — businesses need protocols for AI-to-AI communication that are secure, auditable, and fair.

Personalized AI That Knows Your Business

Current AI tools start every conversation from scratch, or at best, remember limited context from previous conversations. The future is AI that deeply understands your business — your products, your customers, your competitive position, your financial situation, your strategic priorities — and brings that understanding to every interaction.

Some version of this is already possible through custom instructions, knowledge bases, and RAG (retrieval-augmented generation) systems. But the full vision — AI as a genuinely knowledgeable business partner rather than a capable stranger — is still developing.

What this means for your business: Start building the knowledge base a future AI will need. Document your processes, your strategy, your market position, and your institutional knowledge. The companies with this information organized and accessible will get dramatically more value from AI as personalization capabilities improve.

The Cost Curve Continues Down

AI capabilities that cost enterprise budgets today will be available at small business price points within two to three years. This is the pattern with every major technology wave, and there is no reason to expect AI to be different.

What this means for your business: If you are delaying AI adoption because of cost, the economics will only improve. But do not use "it will be cheaper later" as an excuse to avoid learning now. The companies that invest in AI literacy today will capture more value from tomorrow's cheaper, more capable tools.

How to Build an Adaptive AI Strategy

Given all this uncertainty, how do you build a strategy that holds up? By focusing on fundamentals that matter regardless of which technologies emerge.

Principle 1: Invest in People, Not Just Tools

Tools change. The skills to use them well are more durable.

The most important investment you can make is in your team's AI literacy — their ability to communicate effectively with AI, evaluate AI output critically, identify appropriate use cases, and integrate AI into their workflows thoughtfully.

A team with strong AI literacy can adapt to any new tool in weeks. A team without it will struggle even with the best tools on the market.

> Design a quarterly AI skills development program for our team. Focus on transferable skills that will remain relevant regardless of which specific AI tools we use: - Effective prompting and communication with AI systems - Critical evaluation of AI output - Identifying high-value AI use cases in daily work - Ethical and responsible AI use - Data preparation and context-setting for AI tools
>
> Include suggested activities, resources, and success metrics for each quarter.

Principle 2: Build Flexible Infrastructure

Avoid locking yourself into a single AI vendor or platform. The competitive landscape is shifting rapidly, and the best tool today may not be the best tool next year.

Practical steps: - Use API-based integrations where possible rather than deep proprietary integrations that are expensive to replace - Store your data in formats and systems not tied to a specific AI vendor - Train your team on prompting principles that work across platforms, not tricks that only work with one tool -

Maintain active accounts on at least two major AI platforms so you can evaluate alternatives continuously

Principle 3: Document Everything

The businesses that adapt fastest to new AI capabilities are the ones with processes, knowledge, and decision criteria well-documented.

When a new AI capability emerges — say, an agent that can handle your entire invoicing process — the company with that process documented step-by-step can deploy the new capability quickly. The company that relies on institutional knowledge locked in people's heads has to start with process discovery before it can even begin implementation.

Document: - Standard operating procedures for key workflows - Decision criteria for recurring business decisions - Templates and frameworks your team uses regularly - Institutional knowledge that currently exists only in experienced employees' heads - Data dictionaries for your key business systems

Principle 4: Measure Relentlessly

You cannot manage what you do not measure, and you cannot future-proof what you do not understand.

Track AI's impact across your organization. Not anecdotally — systematically.

Metrics that matter: - Time saved per task and per team per week - Quality indicators (error rates, revision cycles, customer satisfaction) - Adoption rates by team and function - Cost per AI-assisted task vs. manual equivalent - Employee satisfaction with AI tools

This data serves two purposes. First, it helps you optimize your current AI use. Second, it gives you a baseline against which to evaluate new tools and capabilities as they emerge. When a vendor tells you their new AI agent will "transform your customer service," you can measure that claim against your actual current performance.

Principle 5: Stay Close to the Technology

You do not need to become a technologist. You do need to stay informed.

Low-effort ways to stay current: - Subscribe to one good AI newsletter (not ten — information overload is counterproductive) - Follow the official blogs of the AI providers you use (OpenAI, Anthropic, Google, Microsoft) - Attend one AI-focused webinar or conference per quarter - Designate someone on your team as the AI scout — the person who tests new tools and reports back on what deserves the team's attention - Use AI itself to stay current: "Summarize the most significant AI developments for business users in the past 30 days"

Principle 6: Start With Reversible Bets

When exploring new AI capabilities, start with experiments that are easy to reverse if they do not pan out.

Good first experiments: - Using a new AI tool for internal tasks before customer-facing ones - Running AI-assisted and manual processes in parallel for a month before switching fully - Piloting with one team before rolling out across the organization - Testing with low-stakes use cases before high-stakes ones

Risky first experiments: - Replacing a core business process with AI without a manual fallback - Signing a multi-year AI vendor contract based on promised features - Automating customer-facing communications without a review period - Making AI-dependent decisions in areas where errors have significant consequences

What Will Not Change

In a chapter about change, it is worth pausing to note what will remain constant.

Critical thinking will still matter. AI will get better at generating analysis and recommendations. The ability to evaluate that analysis, spot its weaknesses, and apply judgment becomes more valuable, not less.

Communication skills will still matter. The better you are at expressing what you want — clearly, specifically, with appropriate context — the more value you will get from AI. This is the same skill that makes you effective with human colleagues, and it is not going away.

Domain expertise will still matter. AI can process information faster than any human. But knowing which information matters, understanding the nuances of your industry, and recognizing when something does not look right — that requires expertise AI complements but does not replace.

Trust will still matter. In an era when AI can produce convincing content on any topic, trust becomes the scarce resource. Trust in your brand, your expertise, your recommendations, and your reliability. Businesses that build trust will outperform businesses that just produce more content.

Ethics will still matter. The ethical principles discussed in the previous chapter are not temporary concerns that better technology will solve. They are enduring responsibilities that grow more important as AI becomes more powerful.

Your 90-Day Future-Proofing Plan

Let me leave you with a concrete plan you can start this week.

Days 1–30: Assess and document. - Audit your current AI usage across the organization - Document your top 10 workflows that AI could enhance - Identify gaps in your team's AI literacy - Review your AI vendor contracts and flexibility

Days 31–60: Build foundations. - Launch an AI skills development program - Begin documenting key processes and decision criteria - Establish measurement systems for AI impact - Evaluate at least one new AI tool or capability

Days 61–90: Expand and optimize. - Based on your measurements, double down on what is working - Test one new use case per team - Create a quarterly review cadence for your AI strategy - Assign the AI scout role to someone on your team

> Create a detailed project plan for this 90-day future-proofing initiative. Include specific tasks, owners, milestones, and success criteria for each phase. Customize it for our context: [describe your organization size, industry, and current AI maturity level].

The Bottom Line

The businesses that will thrive in the AI era share three characteristics: they invest in people over tools, they build systems that adapt to change, and they measure what matters.

You cannot predict exactly what AI will look like in three years. But you can build an organization ready to take advantage of whatever emerges — one with literate people, documented processes, flexible infrastructure, and a culture of thoughtful experimentation.

The future of business AI is not about any single tool or capability. It is about building the organizational muscle to learn, adapt, and improve continuously. Start building that muscle today, and the specifics of tomorrow's technology become much less daunting.

The best time to future-proof your AI strategy was a year ago. The second-best time is right now.

Part VIII: Reference

"If you cannot explain it simply, you do not understand it well enough."

— Albert Einstein (attributed)

Epilogue

When I started writing this book, I had a conversation with a friend who runs a 40-person consulting firm. She had been avoiding AI because she worried it would make her team's work feel less human. Her clients hired her firm for the personal touch, the nuanced thinking, the relationship-driven approach no algorithm could replicate. AI, she thought, would pull her in the opposite direction.

Six months later, she called me again. She had started using AI — reluctantly at first, then enthusiastically. Her team was drafting client deliverables faster, analyzing data more thoroughly, and preparing for meetings more effectively. The result was not less human work. It was more human work. With routine tasks handled more efficiently, her consultants spent more time on what actually mattered: listening to clients, thinking creatively about problems, and building relationships.

"I had it exactly backward," she told me. "AI did not make our work less human. It gave us more time to be human."

That, in a single anecdote, is the thesis of this entire book.

What I Hope You Take Away

If you have read this far — or even if you jumped to this epilogue to see how the story ends — here is what I hope stays with you.

AI is a tool, not a transformation. The transformation is what you do with the tool. A hammer does not build a house — a carpenter with a hammer builds a house. AI does not transform your business — you transform your business, using AI as one of the most powerful tools available.

Start with your work, not with the technology. The question is never "what can AI do?" It is always "what do I need to accomplish, and can AI help me accomplish it better?" Every chapter in this book started with a business task — emails, reports, analysis, strategy — and then showed how AI could improve it. That is the right order.

Good enough today beats perfect next year. AI tools will be better in six months than they are today. Better still in a year. But the benefits start now. The professional who begins experimenting today will be dramatically more effective by the time the next generation of tools arrives. The one who waits for the technology to mature will still be at the starting line.

The human in the loop is not a limitation — it is the point. Every significant example in this book involved a human making decisions: choosing what to ask, evaluating what came back, deciding what to use and what to discard. That is not a temporary phase on the way to full automation. That is the model. Your judgment, your expertise, your values, and your relationships are what make AI output valuable. Without them, AI produces competent mediocrity. With them, it produces something genuinely useful.

Ethics and responsibility are not afterthoughts. The way you use AI reflects your values — as a professional and as an organization. Use it transparently. Watch for bias. Respect other people's data. Take responsibility for the decisions you make with AI assistance. These principles are not a burden. They are what separate the professionals from the amateurs.

One More Thing

I wrote this book with AI assistance. I said so at the beginning, and I want to say it again at the end, because the way I used AI to write this book is exactly the way I am recommending you use it in your own work.

AI helped me research. It helped me draft. It helped me organize my thinking and find better ways to explain complex ideas. But every argument, every recommendation, every opinion in this book came from my experience and my judgment. AI was the capable assistant. I was the author.

That is the relationship I am recommending. Not dependence. Not avoidance. Partnership — where you bring the judgment and AI brings the leverage.

Go Do Something

The best business books are the ones that change what you do on Monday morning. I would rather you take one technique from one chapter and apply it this week than read the whole book and do nothing.

So close this book. Open your AI tool of choice. And do something you have been putting off — draft that difficult email, analyze that spreadsheet sitting on your desk, prepare for that meeting you have been dreading, or think through that decision you have been avoiding.

You now know how to use AI to do it better, faster, and with more confidence than you could alone.

Go.

Appendix A: Use Case Library

This appendix contains 50+ business use cases for AI, organized by department. Each entry includes a brief description, a difficulty rating (Beginner, Intermediate, or Advanced), estimated time savings compared to doing the task manually, and a reference to the chapter where the use case is discussed in detail.

Use this as a quick-reference guide when you are looking for new ways to apply AI in your work, or when someone asks "what else can AI do for us?"

Marketing

#	Use Case	Difficulty	Time Savings	Chapter
1	Draft blog posts from topic outlines	Beginner	60-70%	10
2	Generate social media post variations across platforms	Beginner	50-60%	10
3	Write email marketing sequences	Beginner	50-60%	10
4	Create content calendars (monthly/quarterly)	Intermediate	40-50%	10
5	Analyze competitor content strategy	Intermediate	60-70%	9
6	Write ad copy variations for A/B testing	Beginner	50-60%	10

#	Use Case	Difficulty	Time Savings	Chapter
7	Generate product descriptions for e-commerce	Beginner	70-80%	10
8	Repurpose long-form content into multiple formats	Intermediate	60-70%	10
9	SEO keyword research and content optimization	Intermediate	40-50%	10
10	Analyze campaign performance data and recommend optimizations	Advanced	30-40%	8

Sales

#	Use Case	Difficulty	Time Savings	Chapter
11	Research prospects before meetings	Beginner	50-60%	11
12	Draft personalized outreach emails	Beginner	40-50%	11
13	Write sales proposals and quotes	Intermediate	50-60%	11
14	Prepare for sales calls (objection handling, talking points)	Beginner	30-40%	11

#	Use Case	Difficulty	Time Savings	Chapter
15	Analyze win/loss patterns from CRM data	Advanced	50-60%	11
16	Generate follow-up emails after meetings	Beginner	60-70%	11
17	Create competitive battle cards	Intermediate	40-50%	9, 11
18	Draft case studies from customer data	Intermediate	50-60%	11

Human Resources

#	Use Case	Difficulty	Time Savings	Chapter
19	Write job descriptions	Beginner	60-70%	12
20	Screen resumes against job requirements	Intermediate	50-60%	12
21	Generate interview questions tailored to the role	Beginner	40-50%	12
22	Draft onboarding materials and welcome packets	Intermediate	50-60%	12
23	Write and update employee handbook sections	Intermediate	40-50%	12

#	Use Case	Difficulty	Time Savings	Chapter
24	Create training program outlines	Intermediate	40-50%	12
25	Draft performance review templates	Beginner	50-60%	12
26	Analyze employee survey results for themes and trends	Intermediate	40-50%	12
27	Write internal communications about policy changes	Beginner	50-60%	4, 12

Finance and Accounting

#	Use Case	Difficulty	Time Savings	Chapter
28	Analyze financial statements and identify trends	Intermediate	30-40%	13
29	Categorize and reconcile expenses	Intermediate	40-50%	13
30	Generate budget variance analysis narratives	Intermediate	50-60%	13
31	Draft financial reports and executive summaries	Intermediate	40-50%	6, 13

#	Use Case	Difficulty	Time Savings	Chapter
32	Create financial models and scenario analyses	Advanced	30-40%	13
33	Write board-ready financial presentations	Intermediate	40-50%	7, 13
34	Research tax implications and regulatory changes	Intermediate	30-40%	13

Legal and Compliance

#	Use Case	Difficulty	Time Savings	Chapter
35	Review contracts for key terms and risks	Intermediate	30-40%	14
36	Draft standard contract clauses and templates	Intermediate	40-50%	14
37	Summarize regulatory requirements for a new market	Intermediate	50-60%	14
38	Create compliance checklists	Beginner	40-50%	14
39	Draft privacy policies and terms of service	Intermediate	40-50%	14
40	Research legal precedents and case law	Advanced	30-40%	14

#	Use Case	Difficulty	Time Savings	Chapter
41	Write internal policies (acceptable use, data handling, etc.)	Intermediate	40-50%	14, 21

Operations and Project Management

#	Use Case	Difficulty	Time Savings	Chapter
42	Create project plans and timelines	Intermediate	40-50%	15
43	Write status reports and project updates	Beginner	60-70%	15
44	Conduct risk assessments for projects	Intermediate	30-40%	15
45	Draft standard operating procedures (SOPs)	Intermediate	40-50%	15
46	Analyze operational data for efficiency improvements	Advanced	30-40%	8, 15
47	Create meeting agendas and post-meeting summaries	Beginner	50-60%	5
48	Write RFPs and vendor evaluation criteria	Intermediate	40-50%	15

Strategy and Executive

#	Use Case	Difficulty	Time Savings	Chapter
49	Conduct SWOT, Porter's Five Forces, and other strategic analyses	Intermediate	30-40%	16
50	Analyze market size and growth opportunities	Intermediate	40-50%	9
51	Prepare board presentations and investor updates	Intermediate	40-50%	7, 16
52	Scenario planning and "what if" analysis	Advanced	30-40%	16
53	Summarize industry reports and research papers	Beginner	60-70%	9
54	Draft strategic memos and decision briefs	Intermediate	40-50%	6, 16
55	Evaluate M&A targets (public information analysis)	Advanced	30-40%	16

Cross-Functional

#	Use Case	Difficulty	Time Savings	Chapter

#	Use Case	Difficulty	Time Savings	Chapter
56	Summarize long documents, reports, and PDFs	Beginner	70-80%	6
57	Draft and refine professional emails	Beginner	40-50%	4
58	Translate business documents for international teams	Beginner	60-70%	4
59	Create presentations from raw data or briefs	Intermediate	40-50%	7
60	Build spreadsheet formulas and data transformations	Intermediate	50-60%	8
61	Proofread and edit reports for clarity and tone	Beginner	30-40%	6
62	Generate training materials and how-to guides	Intermediate	40-50%	12, 20

How to Use This Library

1. **Find your department** in the sections above.
2. **Start with Beginner use cases** if your team is new to AI. These require no special setup and produce results quickly.
3. **Move to Intermediate use cases** as your team builds confidence. These usually require sharper prompting skills and more specific context.

4. **Tackle Advanced use cases** once you have established AI workflows and measurement systems. These involve complex data, multi-step processes, or sensitive business decisions.
5. **Track your results.** For each use case you adopt, measure actual time savings against the estimates above. Your numbers may be higher or lower depending on context.
6. **Refer to the listed chapters** for detailed prompts, examples, and best practices.

The time savings estimates assume a user with moderate AI proficiency. Beginners may see lower initial savings that improve with practice. Experienced users often exceed these estimates significantly.

Appendix B: Prompt Templates

These are ready-to-use prompt templates for common business tasks. Copy them, fill in the bracketed sections with your specific details, and use them with any major AI tool (ChatGPT, Claude, Gemini, Copilot, or others).

Each template includes a brief note on when to use it and which chapter covers the topic in depth.

Email and Communication

1. Professional Email Draft

Use when: You need to write an important email and want a strong first draft. (Chapter 4)

> Write a professional email to [recipient and their role] about [topic]. The tone should be [formal/friendly/direct/diplomatic]. Key points to cover: - [Point 1] - [Point 2] - [Point 3]
>
> Context: [Any relevant background the recipient already knows] Desired outcome: [What you want the recipient to do after reading]

2. Difficult Conversation Email

Use when: You need to deliver bad news, push back on a request, or address a sensitive situation. (Chapter 4)

> Help me draft an email to [recipient] addressing [sensitive topic]. I need to: - [What you need to communicate] - [What you want to preserve — relationship, credibility, etc.]
>
> The tone should be respectful but clear. I do not want to be passive-aggressive or vague. The reader should understand exactly [what the situation is / what you are asking] without feeling attacked or dismissed.

3. Email Response to Complaint

Use when: A customer or colleague has sent an unhappy email and you need to respond well. (Chapter 4)

> A [customer/colleague/partner] sent me this email: [paste email]
>
> Help me draft a response that: 1. Acknowledges their concern without being defensive 2. Addresses the specific issues they raised 3. Proposes a concrete resolution or next step 4. Maintains a professional, empathetic tone
>
> Context: [Any additional context about the situation]

4. Internal Announcement

Use when: You need to communicate a change, update, or decision to your team or organization. (Chapter 4)

> Draft an internal announcement to [audience — team, department, all-staff] about [topic]. Key information: - What is changing: [describe] - Why: [the reason behind it] - When: [timeline] - What people need to do: [any actions required] - Who to contact with questions: [name/team]
>
> Tone should be [transparent/positive/matter-of-fact]. Keep it under [word count] words.

Meetings and Collaboration

5. Meeting Agenda

Use when: You are organizing a meeting and need a structured agenda. (Chapter 5)

> Create a meeting agenda for a [duration]-minute meeting about [topic]. Attendees: [list roles/names]. We need to: - [Objective 1] - [Objective 2] - [Objective 3]

> Include time allocations for each section, identify who leads each discussion, and include 5 minutes at the end for action items and next steps.

6. Meeting Summary and Action Items

Use when: You have meeting notes and need to turn them into a clean summary. (Chapter 5)

> Here are my notes from a [type of meeting] with [attendees]. Turn them into a clear meeting summary with: 1. Key decisions made 2. Action items (with owner and deadline for each) 3. Open questions that need follow-up 4. Next meeting date/topic if discussed
>
> Notes: [paste your raw notes]

7. Pre-Meeting Research Brief

Use when: You are meeting with someone and need to prepare quickly. (Chapter 5, 11)

> I have a meeting tomorrow with [person, their role, their company]. Help me prepare a brief that includes: - Company overview (size, industry, recent news) - This person's background and likely priorities - Key topics I should be prepared to discuss - Questions I should ask - Any potential sensitivities or opportunities to be aware of
>
> Context for the meeting: [why you are meeting, what you hope to accomplish]

Reports and Documents

8. Executive Summary

Use when: You have a long document that needs a concise summary for leadership. (Chapter 6)

> Write an executive summary of the following [report/document/analysis]. The audience is [who will read it — CEO,

board, department heads]. They care most about: - [Key concern 1] - [Key concern 2]

Keep it to [length — one page, 500 words, etc.]. Lead with the most important finding or recommendation. Include key data points but skip the methodology unless it is critical to the conclusion.

Document: [paste or upload]

9. Business Report Draft

Use when: You need to write a report and want a structured first draft. (Chapter 6)

> Help me draft a [type of report — quarterly review, market analysis, project update] for [audience]. Structure it with: 1. Executive summary 2. [Section topics] 3. Key findings/results 4. Recommendations 5. Next steps
>
> Data and context: [provide the raw information, data points, and context]
>
> Tone: [professional/analytical/persuasive]. Length: approximately [word count].

10. Proposal Draft

Use when: You are writing a business proposal for a client, partner, or internal stakeholder. (Chapter 6)

> Help me draft a proposal for [what you are proposing] to [who you are proposing it to]. Include: - Problem statement / opportunity - Proposed solution / approach - Scope and deliverables - Timeline - Investment / pricing - Why us / qualifications - Next steps
>
> Key selling points: [what makes this compelling] Known concerns the reader may have: [objections to address]

Presentations

11. Presentation Outline

Use when: You need to build a slide deck and want a strong structure before you start. (Chapter 7)

> Create a presentation outline for a [duration]-minute presentation about [topic] to [audience]. The goal is to [persuade them to / inform them about / get approval for] [specific objective].
>
> Include: - Recommended number of slides - Title and key points for each slide - Suggested data/visuals for each slide - Speaker notes with key talking points - A strong opening hook and closing call to action

12. Talking Points

Use when: You need to present or speak about a topic and want concise, organized points. (Chapter 7)

> I need to present on [topic] for [duration] to [audience]. Create talking points that: - Start with the most important takeaway - Cover [3-5 key themes] - Include specific data points or examples for each theme - Anticipate the top 3 questions the audience is likely to ask and suggest answers
>
> Context: [what the audience already knows, what they care about]

Data Analysis

13. Spreadsheet Analysis

Use when: You have a spreadsheet and need to understand what the data is telling you. (Chapter 8)

> I am uploading a spreadsheet with [describe the data — monthly sales by region, employee survey results, etc.]. Please: 1. Summarize the key trends and patterns 2. Identify any outliers or anomalies worth investigating 3. Create [specific visualizations — bar chart, trend line,

etc.] for the most important findings 4. Highlight the 3-5 most actionable insights 5. Note any data quality issues you observe

14. Dashboard Narrative

Use when: You have data and need to write the narrative that explains it to stakeholders. (Chapter 8)

> Here is our [monthly/quarterly] data for [metrics]. Write a narrative analysis for [audience] that: - Explains what happened and why (to the extent the data supports) - Compares to [prior period/target/benchmark] - Highlights what is going well and what needs attention - Recommends specific actions based on the data
>
> Data: [paste or upload]

Market Research

15. Competitive Analysis

Use when: You need to understand your competitive landscape quickly. (Chapter 9)

> Conduct a competitive analysis of [your company/product] vs. [competitor 1, competitor 2, competitor 3]. For each competitor, analyze: - Product/service offering and key differentiators - Pricing model and positioning - Target market and customer segments - Strengths and weaknesses relative to us - Recent strategic moves (funding, partnerships, product launches)
>
> Our key differentiators are: [list them] Format as a comparison table followed by a narrative summary with strategic implications.

16. Market Sizing

Use when: You need to estimate the size of a market opportunity. (Chapter 9)

> Help me estimate the market size for [product/service] in [geographic market]. Use a top-down and bottom-up approach: - TAM (Total

> Addressable Market) - SAM (Serviceable Addressable Market) - SOM (Serviceable Obtainable Market)
>
> Our product is: [describe] Our target customer is: [describe] Our pricing is approximately: [range]
>
> Show your assumptions and calculations. Flag where you are making estimates vs. using known data.

Marketing and Content

17. Blog Post Draft

Use when: You need a first draft of a blog post. (Chapter 10)

> Write a [word count]-word blog post about [topic] for [target audience]. The post should: - Use a [conversational/authoritative/educational] tone - Include a compelling headline and 2-3 subheadings - Open with a hook that addresses [reader's pain point or question] - Include specific examples or data points - End with a clear takeaway or call to action
>
> SEO target keyword: [keyword] Our brand voice is: [describe]

18. Social Media Campaign

Use when: You need to create a coordinated set of social posts. (Chapter 10)

> Create a [duration — one week, one month] social media campaign for [product launch / event / initiative]. We post on [platforms]. For each post, provide: - Platform-specific copy (respecting character limits) - Suggested image/visual description - Recommended posting time - Relevant hashtags
>
> Campaign goal: [awareness / engagement / conversions] Key message: [the one thing every post should reinforce] Target audience: [describe]

19. Email Marketing Sequence

Use when: You need to create a multi-email nurture or onboarding sequence. (Chapter 10)

> Create a [number]-email sequence for [purpose — onboarding new customers, nurturing leads, re-engaging lapsed users]. For each email, provide: - Subject line (and one A/B variant) - Preview text - Email body - Call to action - Recommended send timing (days after trigger)
>
> Audience: [describe] Tone: [describe] Key conversion action: [what you want them to do]

Sales

20. Prospect Research

Use when: You are preparing for a sales conversation. (Chapter 11)

> Research [company name] for an upcoming sales conversation. I need: - Company overview (size, revenue, industry, key products) - Recent news, press releases, or strategic announcements - Likely pain points based on their industry and size - How our product ([describe briefly]) could address those pain points - Key decision-makers I should try to reach - Potential objections and how to handle them

21. Sales Proposal

Use when: You need to write a sales proposal tailored to a specific prospect. (Chapter 11)

> Draft a sales proposal for [prospect company] for our [product/service]. Include: - Understanding of their needs (based on: [what you learned in discovery]) - Proposed solution and how it maps to their specific requirements - Implementation timeline - Pricing and terms - Case study or reference relevant to their industry - Clear next steps
>
> Their main concerns are: [list known objections or priorities]

22. Follow-Up Email After Meeting

Use when: You just had a sales meeting and need to follow up promptly. (Chapter 11)

> Write a follow-up email after my sales meeting with [name] at [company]. In the meeting: - We discussed: [key topics] - They expressed interest in: [what resonated] - Their concerns were: [objections raised] - We agreed to: [next steps]
>
> The email should reinforce the value proposition, address their concerns briefly, and confirm the next step with a specific date/time.

Human Resources

23. Job Description

Use when: You are hiring and need a well-written job posting. (Chapter 12)

> Write a job description for a [job title] at our company. Details: - Company: [brief description, size, industry] - Department: [which team] - Reports to: [title] - Key responsibilities: [list 5-8] - Required qualifications: [list] - Preferred qualifications: [list] - Compensation range: [if sharing] - Location/remote policy: [specify]
>
> Tone should be professional but reflect our culture, which is [describe]. Avoid jargon and gendered language. Focus on what the person will accomplish, not just what they will do.

24. Interview Questions

Use when: You are preparing to interview candidates. (Chapter 12)

> Generate [number] interview questions for a [job title] position. Include a mix of: - Behavioral questions (past experience) - Situational questions (hypothetical scenarios) - Technical/functional questions specific to [key skills needed] - Culture-fit questions aligned with our values of [list values]
>
> For each question, include what a strong answer looks like and what red flags to watch for.

25. Performance Review Draft

Use when: You need to write performance reviews and want a structured starting point. (Chapter 12)

> Help me draft a performance review for [employee name/role]. Based on the following notes, create a well-structured review that covers: - Overall performance summary - Key accomplishments this period - Areas of strength - Areas for development - Goals for next period
>
> My notes: [paste raw notes, observations, data points] Tone: [supportive/direct/developmental] Rating: [if your system uses ratings]

Finance

26. Budget Variance Analysis

Use when: You need to explain why actuals differ from budget. (Chapter 13)

> Here is our [monthly/quarterly] budget vs. actual data for [department/project/company]. Analyze the variances and: 1. Identify the largest favorable and unfavorable variances 2. Provide likely explanations for each significant variance 3. Flag any variances that suggest a trend vs. one-time events 4. Recommend actions for the variances that need management attention
>
> Data: [paste or upload]

27. Financial Presentation for Board

Use when: You are presenting financial results to the board or executive team. (Chapter 7, 13)

> Create a board-ready financial summary for [period]. Include: - Revenue performance vs. plan and prior year - Key expense variances - Cash flow highlights - Forward-looking guidance and risks - 3 strategic financial topics requiring board input
>
> Data: [provide the numbers] Board's known priorities: [what they care about most right now]

Legal and Compliance

28. Contract Review Summary

Use when: You need to quickly understand the key terms of a contract. (Chapter 14)

> Review this contract and provide a summary of: 1. Key obligations for each party 2. Payment terms and financial commitments 3. Term length, renewal, and termination provisions 4. Liability limitations and indemnification clauses 5. Non-compete or exclusivity provisions 6. Data handling and confidentiality requirements 7. Any unusual or potentially problematic clauses
>
> Flag anything that deviates from standard commercial terms.
>
> Contract: [paste or upload]

29. Policy Draft

Use when: You need to create or update an internal policy. (Chapter 14, 21)

> Draft a [type of policy — AI acceptable use, data retention, remote work, expense reimbursement] policy for our company. Context: - Company size: [number of employees] - Industry: [industry] - Regulatory requirements: [any relevant regulations] - Key objectives of this policy: [what you want to achieve]
>
> Include: purpose, scope, definitions, policy statements, procedures, responsibilities, and enforcement. Keep the language clear and accessible — this will be read by all employees, not just lawyers.

Project Management

30. Project Plan

Use when: You are kicking off a project and need a structured plan. (Chapter 15)

Create a project plan for [project description]. Include: - Project objectives and success criteria - Scope (in scope and explicitly out of scope) - Key milestones and timeline - Resource requirements - Risk assessment (top 5 risks with likelihood, impact, and mitigation) - Communication plan - Dependencies and assumptions

Team size: [number] Duration: [expected timeline] Budget: [if relevant]

31. Status Report

Use when: You need to write a regular project status update. (Chapter 15)

Write a project status report for [project name] for the week of [date]. Based on these notes, create a clear update:

What was accomplished: [list] What is in progress: [list] Blockers or issues: [list] Upcoming milestones: [list] Budget status: [on track / over / under]

Use a Red/Yellow/Green status for overall project health and explain the rating.

32. Risk Assessment

Use when: You need to identify and evaluate risks for a project or initiative. (Chapter 15)

Conduct a risk assessment for [project/initiative]. Identify at least 10 risks across these categories: - Technical risks - Resource risks - Schedule risks - External/market risks - Organizational risks

For each risk, rate likelihood (High/Medium/Low) and impact (High/Medium/Low), describe the potential consequence, and recommend a mitigation strategy.

Strategy and Decision-Making

33. SWOT Analysis

Use when: You need a structured assessment of strengths, weaknesses, opportunities, and threats. (Chapter 16)

Conduct a SWOT analysis for [company/product/initiative]. Context: - Our business: [describe] - Our market position: [describe] - Key competitors: [list] - Recent developments: [anything relevant]

Go beyond the obvious. Challenge my assumptions. For each item, explain why it matters and what we should do about it.

34. Decision Framework

Use when: You are facing a complex decision and need structured analysis. (Chapter 16)

Help me evaluate a decision. I am choosing between: - Option A: [describe] - Option B: [describe] - Option C: [describe]

Evaluate each option against these criteria: - [Criterion 1, e.g., cost] - [Criterion 2, e.g., time to implement] - [Criterion 3, e.g., risk level] - [Criterion 4, e.g., strategic alignment] - [Criterion 5, e.g., team impact]

Rate each option against each criterion, provide a weighted recommendation, and identify what additional information would change the analysis.

35. Strategic Memo

Use when: You need to present a strategic recommendation to leadership. (Chapter 6, 16)

Draft a strategic memo recommending [your recommendation] to [audience — CEO, board, executive team]. Structure: 1. Context — why this decision matters now 2. Options considered — what alternatives were evaluated 3. Analysis — the evidence and reasoning for your recommendation 4. Recommendation — what you propose, specifically 5. Implementation — how it would work 6. Risks — what could go wrong and how to mitigate 7. Ask — what you need from the reader (approval, budget, resources)

Evidence: [provide the data and reasoning you want to include]

AI Workflow and Adoption

36. AI Use Case Assessment

Use when: You are evaluating whether a task is a good candidate for AI. (Chapter 19, 20)

> Evaluate whether [specific task or process] is a good candidate for AI assistance. Assess: - Current time and cost of doing this manually - Frequency (how often is this done) - Skill level required - Risk if AI output is imperfect - Data sensitivity considerations - Available AI tools that could handle this
>
> Provide a recommendation: good candidate, marginal candidate, or not recommended, with reasoning.

37. AI Policy Draft

Use when: Your organization needs an AI acceptable use policy. (Chapter 20, 21)

> Draft an AI acceptable use policy for our organization. Context: - Organization size: [number] - Industry: [industry] - Regulatory environment: [relevant regulations] - Current AI tools in use: [list] - Key concerns from leadership: [list]
>
> Cover: approved tools and tiers, data classification for AI use, disclosure requirements, prohibited uses, review and approval processes, and training requirements. Keep it practical — under 3 pages.

38. AI Training Program

Use when: You are rolling out AI tools to your team and need a training plan. (Chapter 20)

> Design a 4-week AI training program for [team/department]. Current AI proficiency: [beginner/mixed/intermediate]. Goals: - [Goal 1] - [Goal 2] - [Goal 3]
>
> For each week, provide: topic, learning objectives, hands-on exercises, and a way to measure success. Include both individual practice and team exercises.

39. Prompt Library for Your Team

Use when: You want to create a department-specific prompt library. (Chapter 19)

> Create a prompt library of [number] prompts specifically for our [department] team. Our main tasks include: - [Task 1] - [Task 2] - [Task 3] - [Task 4]
>
> For each prompt, include: the prompt template with fill-in-the-blank sections, when to use it, and tips for getting the best results. Organize by task frequency (daily, weekly, monthly).

General Productivity

40. Document Summarization

Use when: You have a long document and need the key points quickly. (Chapter 6)

> Summarize this document. I need: - A 3-sentence executive summary - Key findings or conclusions (bulleted list) - Action items or recommendations (if any) - Anything that surprised you or seems inconsistent
>
> Document: [paste or upload]

41. Research Brief

Use when: You need to quickly get up to speed on a topic. (Chapter 9)

> I need a research brief on [topic] for a business audience. Cover: - Current state of [topic] — what is happening now - Key trends and developments - Major players or stakeholders - Implications for businesses in [our industry] - Sources I should read for deeper understanding
>
> Keep it factual and cite your sources where possible. Flag anything where the information may be outdated or uncertain.

42. Brainstorming Session

Use when: You need fresh ideas and want AI as a thinking partner. (Chapter 16)

> Help me brainstorm [what you need ideas for]. I want: - 10 conventional ideas that are likely to work - 5 unconventional ideas that might be brilliant or might be terrible - 3 ideas that combine approaches from other industries
>
> Context: [describe the problem, constraints, and what has already been tried] Do not self-censor — I want volume and range, not just safe suggestions.

43. Process Documentation

Use when: You need to document a process that currently lives in someone's head. (Chapter 15, 23)

> Help me document our [process name] process. Based on my description, create a clear, step-by-step SOP that a new employee could follow. Include: - Purpose of the process - When to use it (triggers) - Step-by-step instructions - Decision points and criteria - Common exceptions and how to handle them - Who to escalate to and when
>
> My description: [explain the process as you would to a colleague]

Tips for Using These Templates

1. **Customize aggressively.** These templates are starting points. The more specific context you add — your industry, your company size, your audience, your constraints — the better the output will be.
2. **Iterate.** Your first prompt rarely produces the perfect result. Use follow-up prompts to refine: "Make it more concise," "Add more specific data points," "Adjust the tone to be less formal," "Expand the section on risks."
3. **Build your own library.** When you create a prompt that works well for a recurring task, save it. Over time, you will build a personalized library that is more valuable than any book can provide.

4. **Share with your team.** Prompt templates are more valuable when shared. A team that uses consistent, well-crafted prompts produces more consistent, higher-quality outputs.

5. **Update regularly.** As AI tools evolve, some prompting techniques become unnecessary and new ones become possible. Review your prompt library quarterly and update what is no longer working.

Appendix C: Tool Comparison

This appendix covers feature and pricing comparisons for the major AI tools relevant to business users as of May 2026. Pricing and features change frequently — check the vendor's website for current information before making purchasing decisions.

The five tool sections below each list pricing tiers as a stack: each higher tier inherits the previous tier's features and adds what's listed.

General-Purpose AI Platforms

ChatGPT (OpenAI)

- **Free.** GPT-5.5 with limited messages. Limited file uploads and image generation. Web browsing. Custom GPTs: use only, no creation. Training is opt-in (off by default). No admin console, no SSO/SOC 2, no data residency. API requires separate pricing.
- **Plus ($20/mo).** Free plus: full GPT-5.5 + GPT-5.5 mini + GPT-5.x Thinking. Higher message limits. Full file uploads and image generation. Create and use custom GPTs. Same security defaults as Free.
- **Pro ($200/mo).** Plus plus: full GPT-5.5 family with extended Thinking. Near-unlimited message limits. Same security defaults as Plus.
- **Team ($25/user/mo).** Pro plus: admin console. Custom GPTs sharable across team. Training excluded by default. DPA available. SSO/SOC 2 still require Enterprise.
- **Enterprise (custom).** Team plus: SSO/SAML, SOC 2 compliance, data residency options, contractual training exclusion, included API access. Highest message limits.

Best for: Teams that want the broadest feature set and most name recognition. Strong at creative tasks, coding assistance, and general business writing. The custom GPTs ecosystem is the largest.

Watch out for: Pricing adds up quickly at scale. The gap between Team and Enterprise is significant in terms of security features. Even though training is opt-in by default on consumer tiers, settings can be flipped — review them before pasting anything sensitive.

Claude (Anthropic)

- **Free.** Claude Sonnet 4.6 with limited messages. File uploads and 1M context window. Limited Projects. Web search. Training is opt-in (off by default). No admin/SSO/SOC 2.
- **Pro ($20/mo).** Free plus: Sonnet 4.6 + Opus 4.7 + Haiku 4.5. Higher message limits. Full Projects (persistent context). Same security defaults as Free.
- **Max ($100–$200/mo).** Pro plus: extended Thinking, highest consumer message limits. Same security defaults as Pro.
- **Team ($25/user/mo).** Pro plus: admin console. Training excluded by default. DPA available. Higher message limits. SSO/SOC 2 still require Enterprise.
- **Enterprise (custom).** Team plus: SSO/SAML, SOC 2 compliance, contractual training exclusion, included API access, highest message limits.

Best for: Long document analysis, nuanced writing, strategic thinking, and tasks requiring careful reasoning. The large context window makes it the best choice for working with lengthy documents. Strong safety focus means fewer problematic outputs.

Watch out for: Smaller ecosystem of integrations compared to ChatGPT. Image generation requires third-party tools. Less established brand outside tech-forward organizations.

Gemini (Google)

- **Free.** Gemini 3 Flash. Limited Google Workspace integration. NotebookLM included. File uploads. Training is opt-in (off by default). No admin console, no SSO, no data residency.
- **Google AI Plus ($7.99/mo).** Free plus: limited Gemini 3.1 Pro. Limited Gmail and Docs/Sheets/Slides AI features.

- **Google AI Pro ($19.99/mo).** Plus plus: full Gemini 3.1 Pro + 3 Flash. Full consumer Workspace integration including Gmail AI, Docs/Sheets/Slides AI, and Google Meet summaries.
- **Google AI Ultra ($249.99/mo).** Pro plus: full lineup including Gemini 3.1 Pro Deep Think.
- **Workspace Business / Enterprise (priced via Workspace).** Gemini 3.1 Pro across Workspace org-wide. Training excluded by default. Admin console. SSO/SAML and DPA via Workspace. Data residency available.

Best for: Organizations already on Google Workspace. The integration with Gmail, Docs, Sheets, and Meet is seamless and reduces the friction of adoption. NotebookLM is excellent for research and document analysis.

Watch out for: Less capable than ChatGPT or Claude for standalone creative and analytical tasks. Value proposition is weaker if you are not a Google Workspace shop. Business and Enterprise tiers require Workspace subscriptions.

Microsoft Copilot

- **Free (Windows / web).** GPT-5.5 with limits. No Office or Microsoft Graph integration. No admin controls.
- **Microsoft 365 Copilot Business ($18–21/user/mo).** Free plus: GPT-5.5 with Smart / Quick Response / Think Deeper modes. Word/Excel/PowerPoint integration including the agentic Word/Excel/PowerPoint Agents (GA Apr 22, 2026). Outlook and Teams integration. Microsoft Graph access. Copilot Notebooks / Pages / Cowork. Limited Microsoft Foundry agent platform. Admin controls. SSO and DPA via Microsoft 365.
- **Microsoft 365 Copilot Enterprise ($30/user/mo).** Business plus: full Microsoft Foundry agent platform. Standard compliance via Purview. Same Microsoft 365 SSO/data-residency.
- **E7 Frontier Suite ($99/user/mo).** Enterprise plus: priority agent capabilities. Agent 365 included (also $15/user/mo standalone). Entra Suite + advanced Purview compliance.

Best for: Organizations running Microsoft 365. The deep integration with Word, Excel, PowerPoint, Outlook, and Teams is its primary advantage. Microsoft

Graph integration means Copilot can access and reason about your organization's data.

Watch out for: Requires a qualifying Microsoft 365 business plan as a prerequisite. The E7 Frontier Suite at $99/user/month is the most expensive AI seat in the market, justifiable only for organizations going all-in on agentic workflows. Standalone capabilities (without Microsoft 365 integration) are less competitive than dedicated tools.

Perplexity

- **Free.** AI-powered search with source citations. Limited follow-up questions and Pro Search. No file uploads, no API, no team features.
- **Pro ($20/mo).** Free plus: unlimited follow-ups and Pro Search (deeper analysis). File uploads.
- **Enterprise ($40/user/mo).** Pro plus: API access. Team features.

Best for: Research tasks, competitive intelligence, fact-checking, and any task where sourced, current information matters. The citation model makes it easy to verify claims and dig deeper.

Watch out for: Not a general-purpose productivity tool. Less capable for creative writing, document drafting, and data analysis compared to ChatGPT or Claude. Best used alongside a general-purpose AI tool, not as a replacement.

Quick Decision Guide

By Organization Type

- **Microsoft 365 shop, 50+ employees** — Primary: Microsoft 365 Copilot Business or Enterprise. Secondary: Claude or ChatGPT Team for tasks outside Microsoft 365.
- **Google Workspace shop, 50+ employees** — Primary: Gemini for Workspace Enterprise. Secondary: Claude or ChatGPT Team for advanced analysis.
- **Small team (under 20), budget-conscious** — Primary: Claude or ChatGPT Team. Secondary: Perplexity Pro for research.

- **Heavy writing and analysis focus** — Primary: Claude Team. Secondary: Perplexity Pro for research.
- **Broad feature needs, tech-forward team** — Primary: ChatGPT Team. Secondary: Perplexity Pro for research.
- **Research and competitive intelligence focus** — Primary: Perplexity Pro. Secondary: Claude or ChatGPT for other tasks.

By Primary Use Case

- **Email and calendar productivity** — Copilot or Gemini. Native integration with your email platform.
- **Long document analysis** — Claude. Largest context window, strong analytical reasoning.
- **Content creation and marketing** — ChatGPT. Broadest creative capabilities, DALL-E integration.
- **Data analysis in spreadsheets** — Copilot (Excel) or Gemini (Sheets). Native spreadsheet integration.
- **Market research** — Perplexity. Real-time search with source citations.
- **Strategic thinking and planning** — Claude. Strongest reasoning and nuance.
- **Presentation creation** — Copilot (PowerPoint) or Gemini (Slides). Native slide integration.
- **General business writing** — Claude or ChatGPT. Both excellent; Claude edges on tone, ChatGPT on versatility.

By Budget

- **$0/user/mo.** Free tiers of Claude and ChatGPT (do not use for confidential data).
- **$20/user/mo.** One Pro/Plus subscription to your preferred tool.
- **$25–30/user/mo.** Team tier of Claude or ChatGPT.
- **$30–60/user/mo.** Microsoft 365 Copilot or Gemini for Workspace Enterprise plus a standalone tool.
- **$60+/user/mo.** Platform integration (Copilot or Gemini) plus Claude or ChatGPT Team plus Perplexity Pro.
- **$99+/user/mo.** E7 Frontier Suite for organizations standardizing on Microsoft agentic workflows.

Pricing Notes

1. **All prices are as of May 2026** and are subject to change. Check vendor websites for current pricing.
2. **Annual billing** typically offers a 15–20% discount over monthly billing.
3. **Enterprise pricing** is negotiable and often includes volume discounts, dedicated support, and custom terms.
4. **API pricing** is usage-based and separate from subscription pricing. If you are building integrations, budget for API costs independently.
5. **Hidden costs** to consider: training time, workflow redesign, integration development, and the productivity dip during the learning curve. These are real costs even if they do not appear on an invoice.

How to Evaluate for Your Organization

1. **Start with a trial.** Most tools offer free tiers or trial periods. Have 3–5 team members test the top 2–3 candidates on actual work tasks for 2–4 weeks.
2. **Test on your actual tasks.** Generic demos are not useful. Test each tool on the specific types of documents, data, and communications your team works with every day.
3. **Evaluate the security tier you actually need.** Do not buy enterprise features you do not need, but do not use free tiers for sensitive data.
4. **Factor in adoption friction.** The technically best tool is not the best choice if your team will not use it. Integration with existing workflows matters enormously.
5. **Plan for change.** The AI landscape is evolving rapidly. Avoid multi-year commitments unless the discount is substantial and the vendor's roadmap aligns with your needs.

Appendix D: Glossary

A business-focused glossary of AI terms. These definitions prioritize practical understanding over technical precision — the goal is to help you make good decisions about AI in your business, not to pass a computer science exam.

Agentic AI — AI systems that can take a sequence of actions to accomplish a goal, rather than just responding to a single prompt. An agentic AI might research a topic, draft a report, format it, and email it to your team — all from a single instruction. Still emerging in 2026 and requires oversight. (Chapter 23)

AI (Artificial Intelligence) — A broad term for computer systems that can perform tasks typically requiring human intelligence: understanding language, recognizing patterns, making decisions, and generating content. In a business context, this almost always refers to generative AI and large language models. (Chapter 1)

AI Hallucination — When an AI generates information that sounds plausible but is factually incorrect. Examples include citing studies that do not exist, inventing statistics, or confidently stating wrong facts. Hallucinations are less frequent in 2026 models than earlier versions, but they still occur, especially with obscure or technical topics. Always verify critical facts. (Chapter 1)

API (Application Programming Interface) — A way for software systems to communicate with each other. In the AI context, APIs allow businesses to integrate AI capabilities into their own applications, websites, and workflows rather than using AI only through a chat interface. Using APIs typically requires developer resources and is billed based on usage. (Chapter 19)

Bias (in AI) — Systematic patterns in AI output that unfairly favor or disadvantage certain groups. AI bias typically originates from biased training data or biased design choices. In business contexts, AI bias can affect hiring, pricing, customer service, marketing, and other areas with legal and ethical implications. (Chapter 22)

Chatbot — A software application that simulates conversation with users. Modern AI chatbots (like ChatGPT, Claude, and Gemini) are far more capable than the rule-based chatbots of earlier eras, but the term still carries connotations of limited capability. (Chapter 1)

Claude — An AI assistant developed by Anthropic. Known for strong reasoning, nuanced writing, and the ability to work with very long documents. Available in multiple tiers from free to enterprise. (Chapter 2)

Context Window — The amount of text an AI can consider in a single conversation. Measured in tokens (roughly words). A larger context window means the AI can work with longer documents and maintain coherence over longer conversations. As of 2026, context windows range from roughly 100,000 to over 1 million tokens depending on the model. (Chapter 2)

Copilot — Microsoft's AI assistant, integrated into Microsoft 365 applications (Word, Excel, PowerPoint, Outlook, Teams). Uses OpenAI's GPT models. Also available as a standalone chat interface. (Chapter 17)

Custom GPT — A specialized version of ChatGPT configured for a specific purpose, with custom instructions, knowledge files, and sometimes specific capabilities. Businesses use custom GPTs to create AI tools tailored to their specific workflows. (Chapter 19)

Data Classification — The practice of categorizing data by sensitivity level to determine how it should be handled. For AI use, data classification helps determine which AI tools and tiers are appropriate for different types of information. (Chapter 21)

Data Processing Agreement (DPA) — A legal contract between a company and a data processor (such as an AI provider) that governs how personal data is handled. Required under GDPR and increasingly expected in other regulatory frameworks. Enterprise AI tiers typically include DPAs. (Chapter 21)

Deep Learning — A subset of machine learning that uses neural networks with many layers to learn from large amounts of data. Deep learning is the technology underlying modern AI language models. You do not need to understand how it works to use AI effectively in business. (Chapter 1)

Enterprise Tier — The highest level of AI subscription, typically offering the strongest security protections, compliance certifications, admin controls, and contractual guarantees. More expensive but necessary for organizations handling sensitive data or operating in regulated industries. (Chapter 2, 21)

Few-Shot Prompting — A prompting technique where you provide the AI with a few examples of the output you want before asking it to generate its own. Useful for maintaining consistency in format, tone, or style across multiple outputs. (Chapter 19)

Fine-Tuning — The process of training an existing AI model on additional specialized data to improve its performance on specific tasks. Typically requires technical resources and is more relevant for organizations building AI products than for general business use. (Chapter 19)

Foundation Model — A large AI model trained on broad data that can be adapted to many different tasks. GPT-5.5, Claude, and Gemini are foundation models. Think of them as the general-purpose engines that power the specific AI applications you use. (Chapter 1)

Gemini — Google's AI model and assistant, integrated into Google Workspace. Available as a standalone tool and embedded in Gmail, Docs, Sheets, Slides, and Meet. (Chapter 18)

Generative AI — AI that creates new content — text, images, code, audio, video — rather than simply analyzing or classifying existing content. This is the category of AI that has driven the current wave of business adoption. (Chapter 1)

GPT (Generative Pre-trained Transformer) — The model architecture developed by OpenAI that powers ChatGPT. GPT-5.5 and its variants are the current generation as of May 2026. The term is sometimes used generically to refer to any large language model, though this is technically imprecise. (Chapter 1)

Grounding — Techniques that connect AI responses to specific, verified information sources rather than relying solely on the model's training data. Grounding reduces hallucinations and increases factual accuracy. Perplexity's approach to AI search is an example of grounded AI. (Chapter 9)

Guardrails — Constraints built into AI systems to prevent harmful, inappropriate, or off-topic outputs. Business guardrails might include restrictions on generating certain types of content, processing certain types of data, or making autonomous decisions without human approval. (Chapter 20, 21)

Hallucination — See AI Hallucination.

Knowledge Base — A structured collection of information that an AI can reference when generating responses. Businesses can upload internal documents, policies, and data to create knowledge bases that make AI responses more relevant and accurate for their specific context. (Chapter 19)

Large Language Model (LLM) — An AI model trained on vast amounts of text data that can understand and generate human language. ChatGPT, Claude, and Gemini are all powered by LLMs. The "large" refers to the number of parameters (billions) and the volume of training data. (Chapter 1)

Machine Learning — A subset of AI where systems learn from data rather than being explicitly programmed. The AI tools discussed in this book use machine learning, but you interact with them through natural language rather than needing to understand the underlying machine learning processes. (Chapter 1)

Microsoft Graph — Microsoft's system that connects data across Microsoft 365 applications — your emails, documents, calendar, contacts, and more. When Copilot accesses Microsoft Graph, it can reason about your organization's information in context, which is its primary advantage over standalone AI tools. (Chapter 17)

Model — The trained AI system that processes your inputs and generates responses. Different models have different capabilities, costs, and performance characteristics. Choosing the right model for a task is like choosing the right tool for a job — a hammer is not always the right answer. (Chapter 2)

Multimodal — AI that can process and generate multiple types of content — text, images, audio, video, and code — rather than just text. Modern business AI tools are increasingly multimodal, allowing you to upload images, PDFs, and other non-text content for analysis. (Chapter 1)

Natural Language Processing (NLP) — The branch of AI focused on enabling computers to understand, interpret, and generate human language. Every time you type a prompt and get a useful response, NLP is what makes it possible. (Chapter 1)

Parameters — The internal settings of an AI model that determine its behavior. Models are described by their parameter count (billions of parameters). More parameters generally means more capable, but also more expensive to run. As a business user, you do not need to worry about parameter counts — just the practical capabilities they enable. (Chapter 1)

PII (Personally Identifiable Information) — Data that can identify a specific individual: names, addresses, Social Security numbers, email addresses, phone numbers, and similar information. PII requires special handling when used with AI tools, particularly under GDPR, CCPA, and other privacy regulations. (Chapter 21)

Prompt — The text you type to communicate with an AI. A prompt can be as simple as a question or as complex as a multi-paragraph instruction with context, examples, and specific formatting requirements. The quality of your prompt directly affects the quality of AI output. (Throughout the book)

Prompt Engineering — The practice of crafting effective prompts to get the best possible output from AI. While the term sounds technical, it is really about clear communication: being specific about what you want, providing relevant context, and giving the AI enough information to do its job well. (Throughout the book)

RAG (Retrieval-Augmented Generation) — A technique where AI retrieves relevant information from a specified knowledge base before generating its response, rather than relying only on its training data. RAG makes AI responses more accurate and relevant for specific business contexts. (Chapter 19, 23)

Responsible AI — The practice of developing and using AI in ways that are ethical, transparent, fair, and accountable. For businesses, this means considering the impact of AI decisions on customers, employees, and society, not just efficiency and profit. (Chapter 22)

SOC 2 — A compliance framework that certifies an organization's controls for security, availability, processing integrity, confidentiality, and privacy. Enterprise AI tools typically hold SOC 2 certification, which provides assurance about how they handle your data. (Chapter 21)

System Prompt — Instructions given to an AI that define its behavior, personality, constraints, or focus area for a conversation. Custom GPTs and enterprise AI configurations use system prompts to tailor AI behavior for specific business applications. (Chapter 19)

Temperature — A setting that controls how creative or random an AI's responses are. Lower temperature produces more predictable, consistent outputs (good for data analysis and factual tasks). Higher temperature produces more varied, creative outputs (good for brainstorming and content creation). Most business users interact with default temperature settings. (Chapter 19)

Token — The basic unit of text that AI models process. Roughly equivalent to a word, though some words are split into multiple tokens. Tokens matter because they determine how much text an AI can process (context window) and how much API usage costs. A page of English text is approximately 250–300 tokens. (Chapter 2)

Training Data — The massive dataset used to teach an AI model. Training data for current LLMs includes books, websites, articles, code, and other text. The quality and composition of training data affects model capabilities and biases. Importantly, data you share with AI tools may or may not be added to training data depending on your subscription tier and settings. (Chapter 1, 21)

Transformer — The neural network architecture that powers modern LLMs. Introduced in 2017, transformers are what made current AI capabilities possible. You do not need to understand how transformers work to use AI in business — just know that it is the engine under the hood. (Chapter 1)

Zero-Shot Prompting — Asking an AI to perform a task without providing any examples — just a description of what you want. Most casual AI use is zero-shot prompting. It works well for common tasks but may produce inconsistent results for specialized or unusual requests. (Chapter 19)

Appendix E: Resources

The AI for Everyone Series

This book is part of the AI for Everyone series by Finnoybu Press, designed to help real people use AI tools effectively. Each title stands on its own, but together they provide complete coverage of the AI landscape.

Collection 1: Core Tools

ChatGPT: The Definitive Guide (2026 Edition) The comprehensive guide to OpenAI's ChatGPT for power users and professionals. Covers GPT-5.5, custom GPTs, image generation with DALL-E, and advanced prompting techniques.

ChatGPT: The Power User Guide (2026 Edition) Advanced workflows, custom GPTs, and API integration for ChatGPT power users.

Claude: The Definitive Guide (2026 Edition) Everything you need to know about Anthropic's Claude: reasoning capabilities, context windows, artifacts, projects, and how Claude differs from the competition.

Claude Code: The Power User Guide (2026 Edition) Deep dive into agentic development with Claude Code.

Collection 2: Essential Platforms

Gemini: The Complete Guide (2026 Edition) Google's Gemini models, ecosystem, and integrations — both as a standalone tool and integrated across Google Workspace.

Gemini: The Advanced Guide (2026 Edition) Advanced Gemini workflows, multimodal techniques, and Google Cloud integration.

Microsoft Copilot: The Workplace AI Guide (2026 Edition) AI across the Microsoft 365 suite. Covers Copilot in Word, Excel, PowerPoint, Outlook, and Teams, with practical examples and prompts for each application.

Microsoft Copilot: The Advanced Workplace Guide (2026 Edition) Advanced Copilot workflows, automation, and enterprise integration.

Perplexity AI: The Research Playbook (2026 Edition) AI-powered research with real-time citations, source evaluation, and competitive intelligence.

Perplexity AI: The Advanced Research Playbook (2026 Edition) Advanced research workflows, deep analysis, and professional research techniques.

Collection 3: Authoritative Series

AI Systems Playbook (2026 Edition) Architecture, integration, and operations for AI-powered systems.

AI Prompt Engineering (2026 Edition) The complete guide to prompt engineering across models and use cases.

AI for Developers (2026 Edition) Building better software with AI assistants.

AI for Business (2026 Edition) *(this book)* The comprehensive, department-by-department guide to using AI in business, covering every major business function from email to strategy.

AI for Students (2026 Edition) The academic's guide to AI-assisted learning and research.

Official AI Platform Resources

These are the primary documentation and trust resources for the major AI platforms discussed in this book.

OpenAI / ChatGPT - Platform: chat.openai.com - Documentation: platform.openai.com/docs - Trust and Safety: openai.com/safety - Enterprise: openai.com/enterprise

Anthropic / Claude - Platform: claude.ai - Documentation: docs.anthropic.com - Trust and Safety: anthropic.com/research - Enterprise: anthropic.com/enterprise

Google / Gemini - Platform: gemini.google.com - Workspace Integration: workspace.google.com/solutions/ai - Documentation: ai.google.dev - Enterprise: cloud.google.com/ai

Microsoft / Copilot - Platform: copilot.microsoft.com - Microsoft 365 Copilot: microsoft.com/microsoft-365/copilot - Documentation: learn.microsoft.com/copilot - Enterprise: microsoft.com/microsoft-365/enterprise

Perplexity - Platform: perplexity.ai - Enterprise: perplexity.ai/enterprise - Documentation: docs.perplexity.ai

---

AI News and Analysis

Staying current with AI developments does not require reading everything. These sources provide reliable, business-relevant coverage.

Newsletters - *The Rundown AI* — Daily digest of the most important AI news, written for a general audience. Good signal-to-noise ratio. - *Superhuman* — Weekly AI newsletter focused on practical applications and productivity. Business-oriented. - *Ben's Bites* — Daily AI newsletter covering products, research, and industry developments. More technical but accessible.

Publications - *MIT Technology Review* (technologyreview.com) — Thoughtful, well-researched AI coverage. Particularly strong on ethical and societal implications. - *The Verge* (theverge.com/ai-artificial-intelligence) — Accessible technology journalism with strong AI coverage. - *Ars Technica* (arstechnica.com/ai) — More technical but still readable. Good for understanding the "how" behind AI developments.

Podcasts - *Hard Fork* (New York Times) — Weekly technology podcast with regular AI coverage. Accessible and entertaining. - *AI Daily Brief* — Short daily updates on AI developments. Good for staying current without a major time investment.

Privacy and Compliance Resources

International Association of Privacy Professionals (IAPP) - Website: iapp.org - Resource: AI Governance Center — practical guidance for organizations implementing AI

NIST AI Risk Management Framework - Website: nist.gov/artificial-intelligence - The U.S. government's framework for managing AI risks. Increasingly referenced in corporate AI governance.

EU AI Act - Full text and guidance available through the European Commission's digital strategy pages - If you do business in the EU, this legislation directly affects your AI use.

GDPR Resources - Official guidance: gdpr.eu - Particularly relevant: Articles 13, 14, and 22 concerning automated decision-making

---

Books for Further Reading

On AI strategy and business implications: - *Co-Intelligence: Living and Working with AI* by Ethan Mollick — One of the best books on thinking about AI as a collaborative partner rather than a replacement. Mollick's research-backed perspective is refreshingly practical. - *The AI-First Company* by Ash Fontana — Focused on how companies can build competitive advantages with AI. More strategic than tactical.

On AI ethics and society: - *Atlas of AI* by Kate Crawford — A critical examination of the social and environmental costs of AI. Important context for responsible business AI use. - *Weapons of Math Destruction* by Cathy O'Neil — Though published before the current AI wave, its analysis of algorithmic bias remains highly relevant to business AI decision-making.

On prompting and AI communication: - The official documentation from each AI platform (linked above) includes prompting guides and best practices that are regularly updated. These are often more current and practical than books, given how quickly the field evolves.

Community and Professional Development

AI-focused professional communities: - Your industry's professional associations increasingly offer AI working groups and special interest groups. Check your primary professional association for AI-specific resources. - LinkedIn groups focused on AI in specific industries (AI in Marketing, AI in Finance, AI in HR) can be useful for peer learning and staying current with industry-specific applications.

Training and certification: - Google's AI Essentials (available on Coursera) — A solid foundational course for business professionals - Microsoft's AI Skills Initiative — Free training on Copilot and AI productivity tools - LinkedIn Learning — Offers numerous AI for business courses, regularly updated

---

About the Publisher

Finnoybu Press is an imprint of Finnoybu Holdings LLC, focused on practical technology guides for non-technical audiences. Our mission is to help real people use powerful tools effectively — clearly, honestly, and with enough specificity to actually be useful.

Visit **press.finnoybu.org** for: - The latest titles in the AI for Everyone series - Updates and errata for published books - Companion resources and downloadable templates - Bulk licensing options for teams and organizations

For press inquiries, bulk orders, or speaking requests, contact us through the publisher's website.

www.ingramcontent.com/pod-product-compliance
Lightning Source LLC
LaVergne TN
LVHW060029210926
848481LV00013B/3821